CONCRETE TECHNOLOGY

Written by

MANISH KUMAR

SPI Publications

Published by **SPI Publications**, www.spipublications.in

SPI, the **SPI logo**, and **Split Poetry India** are trademarks of **SPI Publications**, or its affiliates.

ISBN-13: 978-93-49860-43-8

First Edition 2025

SPI Publications

Corporate & Editorial Office

117/2, Sector 37, Khandsa Road,
Gurgaon, Haryana 122 001
Phone: +91 98355 52940
Email: contact@spipublications.in
Website: www.spipublications.in

Processed and Printed in India

Preface

Concrete remains the cornerstone of modern construction, shaping everything from buildings and bridges to highways and dams. Its remarkable strength, adaptability, and longevity have made it the most essential material in the civil engineering field. This book, *Concrete Technology*, is a sincere attempt to bridge the gap between theoretical knowledge and practical application, aimed at students, educators and professionals alike.

The content has been structured to align with the needs of diploma and undergraduate civil engineering courses, while also serving as a valuable reference for aspirants preparing for competitive exams. The book covers essential topics such as cement chemistry, aggregate properties, mix design, special concretes, durability and testing methods. Clear explanations, relevant illustrations and updated technical data make the material accessible and applicable.

This work would not have been possible without the guidance and encouragement of several individuals. I would like to express my heartfelt gratitude to my mentors, colleagues and students whose feedback continually shaped the content. Special thanks to My Father Mr. Mahendra Kumar, Dr. Sanjeev Gill HOD Civil Engineering Department, and the editorial support team for their valuable contributions and reviews.

I hope this book proves to be a reliable and enriching resource for all readers, and inspires a deeper understanding of concrete as both a material and a science.

CONTENTS

CHAPTER 1

INTRODUCTION 1-3

CHAPTER 2

CEMENT 4-25

CHAPTER 3

AGGREGATES 26-33

CHAPTER 4

WATER & ADMIXTURE 34-41

CHAPTER 5

MIX DESIGN 42-56

CHAPTER 6

SPECIAL CONCRETE 57-73

CHAPTER 1

INTRODUCTION

Concrete is the most commonly used man-made construction material, valued for its strength, durability, and versatility. Its popularity is not limited to civil engineers — even the general public recognizes its usefulness. One key reason for this is the easy availability of its basic ingredients. Except for cement, components like aggregates and water are readily found in most local areas, making concrete both economical and practical. Because of this, concrete is used in a wide variety of structures — from small pavements to massive expressways, from basic huts to multi-story buildings, and from minor culverts to large, multi-span bridges. Its adaptability to different forms and conditions has made it an essential material in modern construction worldwide.

Developments in Concrete

The widespread use of concrete has led to numerous advancements and innovations in its technology. In the past, we mainly worked with M-20 grade concrete; today, we produce grades well beyond M-60. Where once we relied on conventional concrete, we now have High Performance Concrete (HPC), Ready Mixed Concrete (RMC), and Self-Compacting Concrete (SCC), each with unique characteristics.

Initially, we used only Ordinary Portland Cement (OPC), but today, we utilize blended or cementitious materials — OPC combined with fly ash, slag, and micro silica. Earlier, we focused solely on traditional ingredients like cement, aggregates, and water. Now, we understand the critical role of chemical and mineral admixtures in enhancing concrete performance.

Such remarkable progress has been possible because concrete is now accepted as an ideal construction material. However, this does not mean concrete can completely replace steel or other materials. Instead, it stands alongside them as a viable option, evaluated based on project-specific needs.

There has also been continuous improvement in concrete production methods. Today, we place greater emphasis on material selection, proper proportioning, and the importance of quality control during compaction and curing. These practices have significantly enhanced the overall quality of concrete.

Previously, compressive strength was the sole criterion for judging concrete. Now, we recognize that durability is equally important. Durability ensures long-term serviceability and is influenced by several factors, including water-cement ratio, compaction, and curing. A low water-cement ratio, along with proper compaction and curing, reduces permeability and increases durability.

One significant advancement is Ready Mix Concrete (RMC), produced in controlled batching plants with stringent quality checks. It is transported in truck mixers, maintaining its desired workability until placement.

Another major development is Self-Compacting Concrete (SCC), initially developed in Japan due to labor shortages. SCC flows like a liquid, fills formwork without vibration, and ensures complete compaction even in complex shapes. This not only improves compressive strength but also enhances durability.

To further improve concrete quality, blended cements containing mineral admixtures such as fly ash, slag, and silica fume are now commonly used. Micro silica, due to its ultrafine particles, fills microscopic voids in the concrete matrix, resulting in a highly dense, low-permeability mix. This significantly increases both strength and durability.

Thanks to these innovations and developments, concrete has evolved into a highly reliable and high-performance construction material, playing a crucial role in modern infrastructure.

Production of Concrete

The production of concrete involves two distinct but equally important components: materials and process.

1. Materials

This aspect includes:

- Selection of appropriate raw materials
- Proportioning of materials to achieve the desired concrete mix

2. Process

The process of concrete production includes the following stages:

- Mixing
- Transportation
- Placement
- Compaction
- Curing

Among these, the process plays a more significant role in determining the quality of concrete, even though the cost is mainly influenced by the materials used. While material selection and proportioning are usually handled at higher technical levels, the execution of the process is often left to lower-level staff.

Unfortunately, poor practices in the process—due to ignorance or lack of awareness—can lead to substandard concrete, even if high-quality materials are used. This means that the investment in good materials is wasted if the process is not properly managed.

Therefore, ensuring proper control over the production process can significantly improve the quality of concrete without incurring additional costs. Adopting best practices in mixing, placing, compacting, and curing is essential for achieving strong and durable concrete.

Ingredients of Concrete

The basic ingredients of concrete are:

1. Cement

Cement is the most important and costliest component of concrete. In fact, concrete mix design essentially means optimizing the use of cement to achieve the desired properties in both the fresh (green) and hardened states. Cement significantly influences the overall cost and performance of the structure. Various types of cement are available, each suited for specific structural requirements and environmental conditions. Hence, careful selection of cement is crucial for ensuring the durability and longevity of the structure.

2. Aggregates

Aggregates provide bulk and volume to the concrete, occupying the largest proportion of the mix. Their use enhances the volumetric stability and makes the mix design more economical. Maximizing the quantity of good-quality aggregates is encouraged for better structural performance and cost-effectiveness.

3. Water

Water is essential for the hydration reaction with cement. However, it should be used judiciously—only in the quantity necessary for chemical reaction and workability. Excess water will eventually evaporate, leaving behind capillary pores that weaken the concrete and reduce its durability. Therefore, minimizing water content is key to achieving high strength and long-lasting concrete.

4. Admixtures

Admixtures are optional ingredients used to modify specific properties of concrete, such as setting time, workability, or surface finish. They should not be used to compensate for poor construction practices or low-quality materials. Instead, admixtures are intended to enhance good-quality mixes. In modern concrete types like High Performance Concrete (HPC), Ready Mix Concrete (RMC), and Self-Compacting Concrete (SCC), the use of admixtures has become essential.

CHAPTER 2

CEMENT

History of Cement

Cement is a fundamental binding material in construction, used to bond mineral aggregates together into a cohesive mass. The cement paste, when mixed with water, acts as a glue that holds the aggregates together. This bond is vital, as failure in concrete structures often results from weak bonding rather than weak aggregates.

The invention of modern cement is relatively recent. In 1824, an English bricklayer named William Aspdin patented a material he called *Portland cement*, named for its resemblance to Portland stone. However, the real development of modern cement is credited to Isaac Charles Johnson, who in 1845 produced cement by heating a precise mixture of chalk, clay, and silica to a temperature of 1400–1450°C. At this high temperature, the raw materials fused to form small, greyish-black nodules called clinkers, ranging in size from 3 to 25 mm. On cooling, these clinkers were ground into fine powder—modern cement.

Despite being a 19th-century invention, cementing materials have been used for thousands of years. As early as 2560 BC, the Egyptians used a combination of lime and gypsum to bind stones while constructing the pyramids. The Greeks and Romans used calcined limestone as a cementing agent. These early materials had similar components to modern cement, but they were heated to much lower temperatures, usually below 1000°C, as the technology for higher-temperature kilns did not exist.

One remarkable ancient innovation was pozzolanic cement, named after the town of Pozzuoli in Italy. The Romans created a hydraulic cement by mixing lime with volcanic ash rich in silica and alumina. This blend could set and harden even under water, a property crucial for underwater construction like aqueducts and harbors.

Manufacturing Process of Cement

The manufacturing of Ordinary Portland Cement involves the following key steps:

a) Proportioning and Mixing of Raw Materials

The raw materials (limestone, clay, silica) are **crushed, proportioned, and mixed** to achieve the required chemical composition for cement manufacture.

b) Grinding and Homogenization

The raw mixture is finely **ground and homogenized**, either in dry or wet form, to ensure uniformity in the chemical makeup.

c) Burning in a Rotary Kiln

The prepared raw mix is fed into a **rotary kiln** and heated to a temperature of **1400–1450°C**. At this high temperature:

- **20–30% of the mix melts**, forming a liquid phase.

- The solid particles react chemically and **fuse together** to form hard, greyish-black nodules known as **clinkers**, typically 3–25 mm in diameter.

d) Clinker Cooling and Grinding

After burning, the **clinkers are rapidly cooled** and then **ground with gypsum** (about 3–5%) to regulate the setting time. The final product obtained is **Ordinary Portland Cement**.

The process of cement production is shown in **Fig-1** as a schematic diagram.

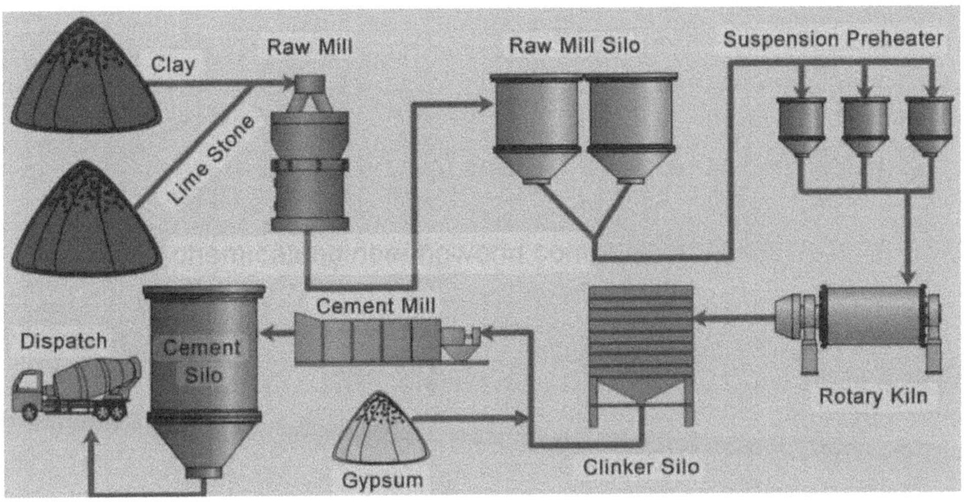

Chemical Composition of Clinker (Approximate)

Table-1

Compound	**Chemical Formula**	**Percentage (%)**
Tricalcium Silicate	C_3S ($3CaO \cdot SiO_2$)	45–60%
Dicalcium Silicate	C_2S ($2CaO \cdot SiO_2$)	15–30%
Tricalcium Aluminate	C_3A ($3CaO \cdot Al_2O_3$)	6–12%
Tetracalcium Aluminoferrite	C_4AF ($4CaO \cdot Al_2O_3 \cdot Fe_2O_3$)	6–10%

Principal Compounds Formed in the Kiln

When the carefully proportioned raw meal is fired in a rotary kiln (≈ 1400–1450 °C), the major oxides (CaO, SiO_2, Al_2O_3, Fe_2O_3) recombine into four principal clinker minerals. A concise summary is given below.

Compound	Cement-chemistry shorthand	Chemical formula	Typical range by mass*
Tricalcium silicate	**C_3S**	$3CaO \cdot SiO_2$	45 – 60 %
Dicalcium silicate	**C_2S**	$2CaO \cdot SiO_2$	15 – 30 %
Tricalcium aluminate	**C_3A**	$3CaO \cdot Al_2O_3$	6 – 12 %
Tetracalcium aluminoferrite	**C_4AF**	$4CaO \cdot Al_2O_3 \cdot Fe_2O_3$	6 – 10 %

Hydration Reactions of the Silicates

On contact with water, these minerals hydrate and harden. The silicates are the chief strength-givers because they form calcium-silicate-hydrate (C–S–H) gel, the nano-structured "glue" of concrete.

1. **Tricalcium silicate (C_3S)**

$$2C_3S+6H \longrightarrow C3S_2H_3+3CH+114 \text{ kJ mol}^{-1}$$

- Products: ≈ **61 % C–S–H** (good) + **39 % $Ca(OH)_2$ (CH)** (less desirable).
- Generates high early heat → rapid early strength but greater risk of thermal cracking.

2. **Dicalcium silicate (C_2S)**

$$2C_2S+4H \longrightarrow C_3S_2H3+CH+43 \text{ kJ mol}^{-1}$$

- Products: ≈ **82 % C–S–H** + **18 % CH.**
- Lower heat evolution, slower early strength, but better long-term strength and durability because more C–S–H and less lime are produced.

Key takeaway: A higher C_2S/C_3S ratio generally improves durability, reduces heat of hydration, and mitigates cracking—important for massive pours and hot climates.

Role of the Other Clinker Minerals

Mineral	Hydration behaviour	Practical effect
C_3A	Reacts very rapidly with water, especially in the presence of dissolved sulphate ions. Gypsum is added at grinding to control (retard) this reaction.	Governs **initial set** and contributes heat but little strength. High C_3A can reduce sulphate resistance.

C_4AF	Hydrates more slowly; heat and strength contributions are modest.	Influences **colour** (grey tint) and slightly reduces energy demand in the kiln because Fe_2O_3 acts as a flux.

Hydration of the Principal Clinker Compounds

1. Hydration of the Silicates (C_3S and C_2S)

Property	**Tricalcium silicate (C_3S)**	**Dicalcium silicate (C_2S)**	**Why C_2S is preferable**
Water required for full hydration	≈ 24 % of cement mass	≈ 21 % of cement mass	Lower mixing-water demand
Heat evolved	High, released quickly	Moderate, released slowly	Lower risk of thermal cracking
C-S-H gel produced	≈ 61 % of products	≈ 82 % of products	Denser, more durable matrix
$Ca(OH)_2$ (CH) produced	≈ 39 % of products	≈ 18 % of products	Less free lime → better durability

Key point: A higher C_2S/C_3S ratio generally yields cooler, less-crack-prone, and more durable concrete, although early strength develops more slowly.

2. Hydration of Tricalcium Aluminate (C_3A)

- **Reaction speed:** Extremely rapid; uncontrolled, it causes *flash set.*
- **Control measure:** 3–5 % gypsum is interground with clinker to form ettringite ($C_6A\check{S}_3H_{32}$), slowing the reaction to allow workable setting times.
- **Strength contribution:** Minimal; hydrated calcium aluminate (C_3AH_6) adds little long-term strength.
- **Durability note:** Excess C_3A lowers sulphate resistance, so its content is limited in sulphate-resisting cements.

3. Hydration of Tetracalcium Aluminoferrite (C_4AF)

- **Quantity:** Minor phase (≈ 6–10 %).
- **Products:** Forms calcium ferrite hydrates (C_3FH_6).
- **Impact:** Generates modest heat and strength. Its main roles are to lower kiln temperature (acting as a flux) and to give cement its grey colour.

Hydration, Strength Gain, and the "Never-Ending" Reaction

- **Early period (first 3 weeks):** ≈ 70–80 % of potential strength is reached as C_3S and part of C_2S hydrate.
- **Long term:** Hydration continues for years, but is progressively hindered because newly formed C-S-H envelops unhydrated clinker grains, restricting further access of water.
- **Practical outcome:** The *theoretical* water demand for complete hydration (~38 % by cement mass) is never fully used. In real mixes, the **water-to-cement ratio** is chosen mainly for **workability**, with the understanding that not all mixing water will participate in hydration; excess remains in capillary pores or evaporates.

Design implication: Specify the lowest w/c ratio that still gives adequate workability. Extra water beyond that point raises porosity and lowers durability without contributing to strength.

Different Types of Cement

A single type of cement may not be suitable for all construction conditions due to variations in environment, structural requirements, and exposure conditions. Therefore, **different types of cement** have been developed to meet specific performance needs.

These modifications are achieved by:

(a) Varying the **oxide composition** of clinker (e.g., reducing C_3A for sulphate resistance),

(b) Altering the **fineness** of grinding (to control early strength gain and reactivity),

(c) Incorporating **additives** or **mineral admixtures** such as **fly ash, blast furnace slag, silica fumes, limestone, or calcined clay**.

Commonly Used Types of Cement

Type of Cement	Key Features	Applications
Ordinary Portland Cement (OPC)	Available in grades 33, 43 & 53 based on compressive strength; fast early strength (especially 53 grade).	General construction, pavements, residential buildings.
Portland Pozzolana Cement (PPC)	Contains 15–35% pozzolanic materials like fly ash or calcined clay; slow strength gain but better durability.	Marine structures, sewage pipes, mass concrete, plastering.
Portland Slag Cement (PSC)	Contains up to 50% granulated blast furnace slag; excellent sulphate resistance and low heat of hydration.	Coastal works, foundations, water-retaining structures.
Rapid Hardening Cement (RHC)	Similar to OPC but more finely ground; achieves strength quickly.	Road repairs, precast works, urgent constructions.
Low Heat Cement	Lower content of C_3A and C_3S; reduces heat generation during hydration.	Dams, massive foundations, retaining walls.

Sulphate Resisting Cement	Low C_3A content; improves resistance to sulphate attack.	Sewage treatment plants, marine and industrial structures.
White Cement	Free from iron oxide; white in colour.	Decorative works, tile grout, flooring, architectural finishes.
Coloured Cement	White cement base mixed with pigments.	Flooring, decorative facades.
Expansive Cement	Expands slightly on setting, preventing shrinkage cracks.	Grouting, repairs, anchoring bolts.
Hydrophobic Cement	Contains additives to repel moisture during storage.	Construction in damp climates or where storage conditions are poor.

Recent Innovations in Cement Types

Innovation	Description	Benefit
Geopolymer Cement	Made from industrial waste like fly ash and activated using alkaline solutions (no limestone/clinker).	80–90% lower CO_2 emissions; high chemical resistance.
CarbonCure™ Cement	CO_2 is injected into concrete during mixing and becomes mineralized.	Permanent CO_2 storage, increased strength, greener concrete.
LC^3 (Limestone Calcined Clay Cement)	Partially replaces clinker with a blend of calcined clay and limestone.	Cuts carbon footprint by up to 40%; cost-effective and durable.
Photocatalytic Cement	Contains titanium dioxide that breaks down air pollutants under sunlight.	Self-cleaning and air-purifying surfaces.
Self-healing Cement	Embedded capsules or bacteria activate upon cracking to seal cracks automatically.	Enhanced durability and lower maintenance.

1. Ordinary Portland Cement (OPC)

Ordinary Portland Cement (OPC) is the most widely used cement in general construction work. The term "Portland" comes from its resemblance, after setting, to a type of building stone known as Portland Stone, quarried in Dorset, UK.

In India, OPC is available in three grades based on its compressive strength after 28 days (tested as per IS 4031):

- **Grade 33**: Minimum 28-day strength = 33 MPa
- **Grade 43**: Minimum 28-day strength = 43 MPa
- **Grade 53**: Minimum 28-day strength = 53 MPa

Higher grades mean faster strength gain, but also higher heat of hydration. Grade selection should depend on structural requirement and environmental exposure.

2. Rapid Hardening Cement (RHC)

Rapid Hardening Cement (RHC) is also known as Early Strength Cement, as it gains strength significantly faster than OPC. The 3-day compressive strength of RHC is nearly equivalent to the 7-day strength of OPC.

RHC should not be confused with Quick Setting Cement, which only sets quickly but does **not** gain strength rapidly.

Reasons for Faster Strength Gain in RHC:

1. **Higher Fineness**:

- Specific surface area ≈ **320 m²/kg**
- Compared to ≈ **225 m²/kg** for normal OPC
- Increased surface area enhances the reaction rate with water.

2. **Higher C_3S Content**:

- Tricalcium silicate (C_3S) hydrates faster than C_2S and contributes to early strength.
- RHC has a higher percentage of C_3S compared to ordinary OPC.

Precautions:

Due to its high early heat of hydration, RHC should **not be used** in:

- **Mass concrete structures** with low surface-area-to-volume ratio
- Projects where **thermal cracking** is a concern

Recommended Applications:

- Pre-fabricated structures, where early demolding is essential
- Quick repair work, especially in road pavements
- Cold weather concreting, where heat evolution helps prevent freezing
- Situations where early load-bearing strength is critical, such as in high-speed construction

3. Sulphate-Resistant Cement (SRC)

Sulphate-Resistant Cement is a specially formulated Portland cement designed to minimise internal expansion and cracking when concrete is exposed to sulphate-bearing soils, ground-water, or industrial effluents.

3.1 Why ordinary OPC fails in sulphate environments

- **Abundant free lime:**
  Ordinary Portland cement (OPC) hydration liberates calcium hydroxide, **$Ca(OH)_2$**.
- **Reaction with sulphate ions:**
  External sulphate ions (SO_4^{2-}), especially from magnesium sulphate ($MgSO_4$) or sodium sulphate (Na_2SO_4), react with $Ca(OH)_2$ to form gypsum **($CaSO_4{\cdot}2H_2O$).**
- **Formation of expansive ettringite:**
  Gypsum then reacts with the hydrates of tricalcium aluminate to form calcium sulpho-aluminate (ettringite, $C_3A{\cdot}3CaSO_4{\cdot}32H_2O$). Ettringite occupies a much larger volume than the original hydrate, producing internal stresses that cause cracking and spalling.
- **Marine "tidal-zone" acceleration:**
  Alternate wetting and drying cycles common in tidal or splash zones pump sulphate ions into the concrete and concentrate them as water evaporates, intensifying damage.

3.2 How sulphate-resistant cement is made

The key is to **limit the aluminates** that produce ettringite:

Limiting parameter	Target for SRC	Typical OPC value
C_3A content	**< 5 %** (IS 12330 / ASTM C150 Type V)	8 – 12 %
3 C_3A + C_4AF	**< 25 %** (empirical durability guideline)	30 – 40 %

3.3 Practical tips for specification and use

- **Verify exposure class** (e.g., per IS 456 or ACI 318) and match the cement to the sulphate concentration in soil/water.
- Combine SRC with **low water-to-cement ratio**, good compaction, and adequate curing for a dense, impermeable matrix.
- **Supplementary cementitious materials** (slag, fly-ash, silica fume) further lower permeability and improve sulphate resistance.
- For mass pours, check the heat of hydration; SRC typically produces *slightly* less heat than OPC but not as low as dedicated low-heat cement.

4. Blast Furnace Slag Cement (GGBFS Cement)

Blast Furnace Slag Cement is made by mixing Ordinary Portland Cement (OPC) clinker with blast furnace slag (a waste from steel industry) and gypsum. Usually, 25% to 65% slag is used. This slag is ground with the clinker to make cement.

4.1 Manufacturing routes

Route	Description	Comment
Inter-grinding	Clinker, granulated slag, and gypsum are ground together in a finish mill.	Gives most uniform product; normal commercial method.
Separate grinding & blending	Slag is ground to GGBFS, stored separately, and blended with OPC at the batching plant.	Flexible for ready-mix plants but requires precision metering and high-shear mixers for full dispersion.

4.2 Why use slag? – Performance & sustainability

Attribute	Effect
Lower heat of hydration	Safer for mass concrete and hot-weather pours.
Improved durability	Higher resistance to sulphate, chloride, alkali–silica reaction, and soft-water leaching.
Later-age strength gain	Slower early strength, but equal or higher 90-day and ultimate strength.
Enhanced workability	Finer particle shape and latent-hydraulic reaction act like a plasticiser.
Sustainability	Each tonne of granulated slag used in place of clinker saves ~0.8 t of CO_2 and conserves lime and fuel.

4.3 Typical applications

- **Sewage and waste-water treatment plants** – superior sulphate and biogenic acid resistance.
- **Marine and coastal structures** – combined chloride- and sulphate-rich environments.
- **Mass concrete pours** – rafts, dams, thrust blocks, where low heat rise mitigates thermal cracking.
- **Water-retaining structures** – reservoirs, treatment tanks, where leaching resistance is needed.
- **Industrial floors & chemical plants** – better resistance to mild acids and alkalis.

5. Portland Pozzolana Cement (PPC)

Portland Pozzolana Cement, commonly referred to as PPC, is a modern blended cement that is gaining wide popularity due to its environmental benefits, improved durability, and long-term performance. It is manufactured by blending Ordinary Portland Cement (OPC) clinker with pozzolanic materials such as fly ash, volcanic ash, calcined clay, or silica fumes, along with a small quantity of gypsum.

The term *'pozzolana'* is derived from a natural volcanic ash found in Pozzuoli, Italy, near Mount Vesuvius. These materials, though not cementitious by themselves, exhibit cement-like properties when finely divided and mixed with calcium hydroxide ($Ca(OH)_2$) in the presence of water. The chemical reaction that takes place produces strong binding compounds, similar to those formed during the hydration of OPC.

5.1 Pozzolanic Reaction and Strength Development

In the hydration process of OPC, compounds like tricalcium silicate (C_3S) react with water to produce calcium silicate hydrate (C-S-H) gel and calcium hydroxide ($Ca(OH)_2$). The pozzolanic materials present in PPC utilize this free lime to form additional C-S-H gel, thereby increasing the density and strength of the concrete.

The main chemical reactions involved are as follows:

$2C_3S+6H \rightarrow C_3S_2H_3+3CH$

(Primary hydration of OPC)

$CH+SiO_2+H_2O \rightarrow C-S-H$ (Pozzolanic Reaction)

This additional gel formation not only strengthens the concrete but also reduces porosity, making the structure more durable and less permeable to water and aggressive chemicals.

5.2 Manufacturing and Materials Used

PPC is produced either by inter-grinding pozzolanic materials with OPC clinker or by blending the two separately and then grinding the mixture. Fly ash, a by-product of coal-fired thermal power plants, is the most commonly used pozzolana in India due to its wide availability and quality.

To ensure proper blending and fineness, the pozzolana used must meet certain quality standards. According to IS: 3812 (Part 1) – 2013, the combined percentage of silica and alumina in fly ash must be at least 70%, and the loss on ignition should not exceed 12%.

The typical fineness of fly ash used in PPC is around 300 m^2/kg, which is higher than the fineness of OPC (225 m^2/kg), allowing better reaction and blending.

5.3 Advantages of PPC

Portland Pozzolana Cement offers several advantages over traditional OPC, particularly in terms of long-term performance and sustainability. These include:

1. **Lower Heat of Hydration:** The pozzolanic reaction is slower, reducing the risk of thermal cracking in mass concrete works such as dams or retaining walls.
2. **Improved Durability:** The concrete becomes denser and less permeable, offering better resistance to sulphate attack, chloride ingress, and alkali-aggregate reaction.
3. **Utilization of Industrial Waste:** PPC makes use of fly ash and other pozzolanic materials, reducing the burden on landfills and promoting eco-friendly construction.
4. **Reduced Lime Leaching:** The use of pozzolana consumes free $Ca(OH)_2$, minimizing efflorescence and improving the concrete's resistance to chemical attacks.
5. **Cost-Effectiveness:** In many regions, PPC is more economical than OPC due to the use of industrial by-products.

5.4 Typical Strength Characteristics

PPC gains strength more slowly than OPC in the early days, but continues to develop strength over time. The initial strength is mainly due to the OPC content, while the pozzolanic materials begin contributing after 7 days.

- **7-day compressive strength:** ≥ 22 MPa
- **28-day compressive strength:** ≥ 31 MPa

Despite the slower early strength gain, PPC is preferred in many situations for its superior long-term performance and durability.

5.5 Applications and Recommended Use

PPC can be used in almost all types of construction works where OPC is traditionally used. However, its use is particularly advantageous in the following situations:

- Mass concrete structures like dams, canals, and retaining walls
- Marine structures, sewage treatment plants, and water tanks
- Road pavements, bridges, and residential buildings
- Construction in aggressive environments (sulphate or chloride rich soils)

Its improved resistance to chemical attacks and low permeability make it ideal for these environments.

6. Air Entraining Cement

Air Entraining Cement is a special type of cement in which air is intentionally introduced in the form of tiny, uniformly distributed air bubbles. These bubbles improve the properties of both fresh and hardened concrete, making it more workable, durable, and frost-resistant.

The air bubbles function like soft, flexible ball bearings that reduce internal friction among the components of concrete—cement, water, sand, and aggregates. As a result, the workability of concrete improves even without increasing the water content. This is especially useful in harsh climates and large concrete structures where durability and frost resistance are critical.

6.1 Air Content and Performance

The ideal air content in air-entrained concrete is typically between **3% to 6%** by volume of the concrete mix. Proper air entrainment leads to improvements in:

- **Fresh Concrete:**
    - Improved workability
    - Reduced bleeding and segregation
    - Better surface finish
- **Hardened Concrete:**
    - Increased resistance to **frost and freeze-thaw cycles**

- Reduced **permeability**, which protects against water and chemical ingress

This makes air entraining cement particularly useful in **cold climates** or where the concrete may be exposed to frequent freezing and thawing.

Air Entraining Agents

Air entrainment is achieved by adding certain chemical admixtures known as **air entraining agents**. These are mixed either during the manufacturing of cement or directly during concrete mixing. Commonly used agents include:

- **Alkali salts of wood resin**
- **Synthetic detergents**
- **Calcium lignosulphonate**
- **Aluminium powder and animal fats**

These agents are also sold under commercial trade names such as Vinsol Resin, Airlon, Darex, and Teepol.

Entrained Air vs. Entrapped Air

It is important to distinguish between entrained air and entrapped air, as they have very different effects on concrete quality. The following table explains the differences:

Table 3: Difference Between Entrained and Entrapped Air

Entrained Air	Entrapped Air
1. Intentionally introduced and evenly distributed.	1. Accidental, caused by poor compaction, and unevenly distributed.
2. Bubble size is very small, typically **5–80 µm**.	2. Pockets may be large, varying from **10–1000 µm**.
3. Bubbles are spherical in shape.	3. Irregular shapes depending on aggregate surfaces.
4. Beneficial for durability and workability.	4. Harmful; reduces concrete strength and performance.

6.2 Use in India and Historical Relevance

Air Entraining Cement has not gained much popularity in India and is not currently covered under any Indian Standard (IS) code. However, it was used in several major concrete structures during the mid-20th century. Notably, large-scale dam projects like:

- **Hirakud Dam**
- **Koyna Dam**

- **Rihand Dam**

used air entraining agents like Vinsol and Darex, which were imported from the USA at that time. These projects highlighted the usefulness of air entrained concrete in enhancing durability and reducing long-term maintenance, especially in water-retaining and temperature-sensitive structures.

7. Quick Setting Cement

Quick Setting Cement is a special type of cement that sets much faster than Ordinary Portland Cement (OPC). Normally, gypsum is added during cement manufacturing to control the setting time of cement. However, in Quick Setting Cement, a smaller amount of gypsum is added—or in some cases, not added at all.

This reduction in gypsum allows the cement to set quickly after coming in contact with water. While the initial setting time is very short, the final strength is still developed over time like ordinary cement.

Applications of Quick Setting Cement

This cement is especially useful in:

- Underwater or flowing water construction
- Grouting operations
- Situations where fast setting is needed due to limited working time

Quick setting cement must be handled carefully and placed immediately after mixing, as any delay can cause setting before placing or finishing.

8. Expansive Cement

Most types of cement tend to shrink as they dry and harden. This drying shrinkage can lead to cracking and may affect the durability of concrete. To avoid this problem, Expansive Cement is used.

Expansive Cement is made by adding compounds like sulpho-aluminates, which expand slightly after setting. This small expansion helps to counteract the shrinkage that naturally occurs, keeping the volume of the concrete nearly constant.

Uses of Expansive Cement

This type of cement is recommended for:

- Repair works where cracking due to shrinkage must be avoided
- Grouting anchor bolts
- Sealing joints in water-retaining structures
- Construction of large slabs or pavements where shrinkage could cause visible cracks

9. High Alumina Cement (HAC)

High Alumina Cement is a fast-setting and high-strength cement made using lime and bauxite as the main raw materials. Because bauxite is rich in alumina (Al_2O_3), this cement contains a high percentage of alumina—hence the name.

One of its key features is its very rapid strength gain. It can achieve up to 80% of its full strength within 24 hours. This is much faster than Ordinary Portland Cement or even Rapid Hardening Cement.

However, this fast strength gain also means a large amount of heat is released—up to 2.5 to 3 times that of Rapid Hardening Cement. Therefore, formwork should be removed early to avoid heat build-up and possible thermal cracks.

Advantages of High Alumina Cement

- Rapid strength development
- High resistance to sulphate attack
- Absence of $Ca(OH)_2$, making it more chemically stable
- Useful in cold weather conditions where early strength is essential

Common Applications

- Emergency repair works
- Industrial flooring
- Chemical plants and sewer works
- Marine structures exposed to sulphates

Tests of Cement

To ensure the quality and performance of cement before use in construction, various tests are conducted. These tests can be broadly divided into two categories:

A) Field Tests
B) Laboratory Tests

A) Field Tests of Cement

Field tests are simple checks performed on-site to get a rough idea of the quality of cement without the need for laboratory equipment. These tests are useful when quick decisions are needed on the spot.

1. Date of Manufacture

Always check the **manufacturing date** printed on the cement bag. Cement loses its strength over time, so it should ideally be used fresh. A general idea of how strength reduces with time is shown below:

Storage Period	Strength (Compared to Fresh Cement)
Fresh	100%
3 months	80%
6 months	70%
12 months	60%
24 months	50%

2. Visual Inspection for Lumps

Open the bag and check the cement. It should be free from hard lumps. Presence of lumps indicates that moisture has entered the bag and partial setting may have occurred.

3. Touch Test

Put your hand into the cement bag. It should give a cool feeling, which means that no hydration (chemical reaction with water) is taking place inside the bag.

4. Fineness and Texture

Take a small pinch of cement between your fingers and rub it. It should feel smooth and fine. If it feels gritty, the cement may not be properly ground or may be contaminated.

5. Float Test

Throw a **handful of cement** on the surface of still water in a bucket. Good quality cement will **float for a few moments** before gradually sinking. If it sinks immediately, the cement may have lost its quality.

6. Cake Test (Setting Test in Water)

Take about 100 grams of cement and mix it with a small amount of water to form a stiff paste. Make a cake or patty with sharp edges and place it on a glass plate. Then gently immerse the plate in water.

- The cement cake should retain its shape and set properly without disintegrating.
- This test demonstrates that the cement has hydraulic properties, meaning it can set and gain strength under water.

B) Laboratory Tests of Cement

Although most cement manufacturers carry out detailed testing in their own laboratories and provide a test certificate with every supply, it is still important for users or construction agencies to perform some basic laboratory tests.

These tests help in:

- Verifying the authenticity and quality of the cement received.
- Checking for any loss of strength or deterioration during transport and storage.
- Ensuring that the cement meets the required IS standards and specifications.

a. Fineness of Cement

The fineness of cement plays a very important role in the rate of reaction between cement and water, which is called the hydration reaction. Finer cement means smaller particles, which increases the surface area available for reaction. As a result, cement hydrates faster, gains strength earlier, and also produces more heat during hydration.

Why Fineness is Important

- Finer cement sets and gains strength faster, which is useful in urgent construction or cold weather.
- It helps in better bonding in mortar and concrete.
- Too coarse cement hydrates slowly and may reduce early strength.

How Fineness is Measured

Fineness of cement can be tested in two main ways:

1. **Sieve Test**
- Cement is passed through a **90-micron sieve**.
- The leftover residue on the sieve is measured.
2. **Specific Surface Area Test** (Air Permeability Method)
- This test measures the surface area of cement particles per kilogram.
- It is expressed in square meters per kg (m^2/kg).

IS Code Requirements

According to **IS 4031**:

Type of Cement	Sieve Residue Limit	Minimum Specific Surface
Ordinary Portland Cement (OPC)	Less than 10%	225 m^2/kg
Portland Pozzolana Cement (PPC)	Less than 5%	320 m^2/kg
Slag Cement (SGC)	Less than 5%	375 m^2/kg

Effect of Fineness on Cement Properties

1 **Faster Reaction:** Finer cement reacts quickly with water and leads to faster setting and early strength gain.

2 **More Heat of Hydration:** Because the reaction is faster, more heat is released in the early stage. This may be helpful in cold weather but can cause cracking in large pours if not controlled.

3 **Ultimate Strength Remains Same:** Although strength gains are quicker, the final strength after 28 days does not increase significantly with fineness.

Relation between specific surface and strength

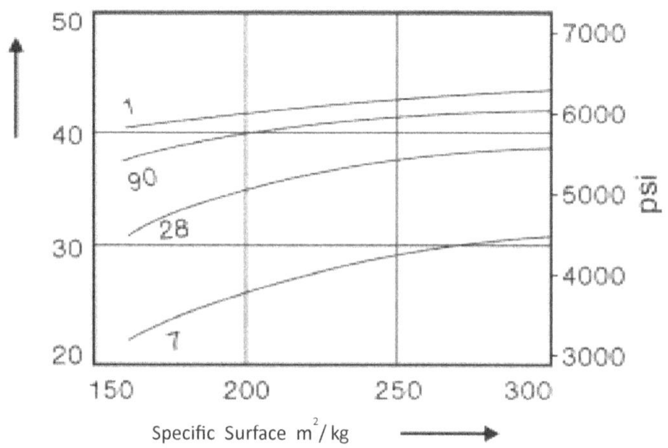

From this figure it is evident that 7 days or 28 days strength may be higher for finer cement but 1 year strength is almost same even for higher fineness. In fact it will be exactly same if we compare the ultimate strength at infinity.

(1) Chance of bleeding reduces in the concrete if finer cement is used.

(2) Shrinkage and cracking in the concrete increases with fineness.

Note: 'Bleeding' is the separation of water from cement paste and 'segregation' means separation of aggregates from the concrete.

b. Standard Consistency Test of Cement

The Standard Consistency Test does not directly assess the quality of cement. Instead, it helps determine the amount of water required to make a cement paste of standard consistency. This consistency is essential for conducting other important tests such as:

- Initial setting time
- Final setting time
- Soundness
- Compressive strength

By determining the correct amount of water to be added, we ensure that these tests are accurate and consistent.

Apparatus Used: Vicat's Apparatus

The test is conducted using the Vicat's Apparatus, which consists of:

- A movable rod with a plunger (10 mm diameter and 50 mm length)
- A graduated scale to measure penetration
- A split mould (Vicat mould), 80 mm in height and 70 mm in diameter
-

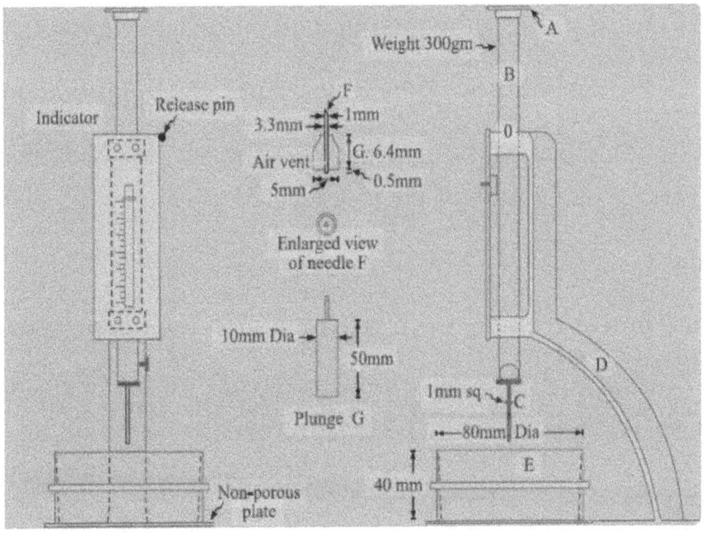

Test Procedure

1. Take 300 grams of cement.
2. Add about 25% water by weight of cement and mix thoroughly to form a uniform paste.
3. Fill the paste into the Vicat mould placed on a non-porous plate.
4. Lower the plunger gently so it touches the surface of the paste.
5. Release the plunger and allow it to penetrate into the cement paste freely.
6. Observe the depth of penetration:
   - If the plunger stops 5 to 7 mm above the bottom of the mould, the paste has the standard consistency.
7. If not, repeat the process with a slightly adjusted amount of water (increase or decrease), until the desired penetration is achieved.

c. Setting Time Tests

Setting time refers to the time taken by a cement paste to transition from a fluid or plastic state to a hardened state. It is an essential parameter for handling, placing, and finishing concrete or mortar.

Two setting times are defined:

(i) Initial Setting Time

- The initial setting time is the duration from the moment water is added to the cement until the paste begins to lose its plasticity.
- This is measured using the Vicat's apparatus, fitted with a 1 mm^2 needle.
- The test is conducted under controlled temperature conditions of 27 ± 2°C.
- A paste is made by adding 0.85 × P amount of water to 500 g of cement, where 'P' is the percentage of water determined by the standard consistency test.
- The needle is allowed to penetrate the cement paste at regular time intervals.
- The initial setting time is the time elapsed when the needle penetrates the paste and stops at 5 ± 0.5 mm above the bottom of the mould.

(ii) Final Setting Time

- The final setting time is the time from water addition until the paste completely loses its plasticity and becomes rigid.
- This part of the test continues using a modified needle with a circular cutting edge around the main needle.
- When penetration is more than 0.5 mm, both the needle and the ring leave impressions on the paste.
- When only the needle makes an impression (and the ring does not), it indicates that the paste has hardened.
- This moment marks the final setting time.

Table: Summary of Setting Time Test

S. No.	Setting Type	Definition	Needle Type	Standard Limit (OPC)
1	Initial Setting Time	Time when needle penetrates up to **5 ± 0.5 mm** from the bottom	1 mm^2 needle	≥ 30 minutes
2	Final Setting Time	Time when **circular ring fails to leave an impression** on the paste	Needle with circular cutting ring	≤ 600 minutes (10 hrs)

d. Soundness Test

The soundness test is performed to determine the presence of excess free (unburnt or hard-burnt) lime in cement. Excess lime can lead to undesirable expansion after the cement has set, resulting in cracking and loss of durability.

During the manufacturing of cement, if lime does not properly combine with acidic oxides during burning in the kiln, free lime (CaO) may remain. This lime hydrates slowly and may only react after the cement has hardened. When hydration of this free lime occurs, it forms calcium hydroxide [$Ca(OH)_2$], which occupies a greater volume than the original quicklime. Since hardened cement does not provide space for expansion, the result is internal stress and cracking, a condition referred to as the unsoundness of cement.

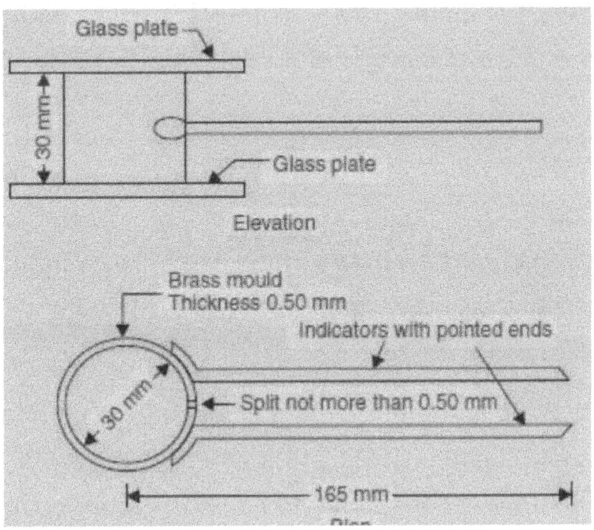

Causes of Excess Free Lime in Cement:

1. Inadequate burning of raw materials
2. Insufficient grinding of raw materials
3. Improper mixing of raw materials

The degree of expansion caused by free lime is an indicator of soundness. Cement is considered sound if this expansion is within permissible limits; otherwise, it is unsound.

The expansion is measured using the Le Chatelier Apparatus.

- For ordinary cements, the maximum allowed expansion is 10 mm.
- For Special Grade Cement (SGC), the limit is 5 mm.

Test Procedure for Soundness Test:

Step 1: Prepare a cement paste by mixing cement with water in the ratio of $0.78 \times P$, where P is the percentage of water required for standard consistency.

Step 2: Fill the paste into a Split Brass Mould (30 mm internal diameter and 30 mm height), which is split vertically and fitted with a 165 mm-long indicator arm to magnify any expansion.

Step 3: Cover the mould with glass plates on both the top and bottom surfaces.

Step 4: Place the entire assembly in water maintained at a temperature of 27°C to 32°C.

Step 5: After 24 hours, remove the mould from the water and measure the distance between the indicator ends. Let this distance be denoted as 'x'.

e. Strength Test

The strength test is performed to determine the compressive strength of cement, which is a key indicator of its quality and performance.

In this test, a cement-sand paste is prepared in a 1:3 ratio (cement : standard sand). Sand is used to reduce the shrinkage of the cement paste during setting and hardening.

Mix Proportions:

- **Cement**: 200 g
- **Standard Sand**: 600 g
- **Water**: (P/4)+3.0(P/4) + 3.0(P/4)+3.0% of the combined weight of cement and sand, where **P** is the percentage of water required for standard consistency.

Procedure:

1. Mix the ingredients thoroughly for 3–4 minutes to form a uniform paste.
2. Fill the paste into cube moulds of size 7.06 cm × 7.06 cm × 7.06 cm.
3. Compact the paste using a standard vibrating table.
4. Keep the moulds in a moist atmosphere (at 27 ± 2°C and 90% relative humidity) for 24 hours.
5. After 24 hours, remove the cubes from the moulds and submerge them in clean fresh water maintained at 27 ± 2°C.
6. Test the compressive strength of the cubes after 1, 3, 7, and 28 days, depending on the type of cement.

For each age, three cubes are tested, and the average compressive strength of the three cubes is reported as the result. A fresh batch of material is prepared separately for each set of three cubes.

f. Loss on Ignition Test

The Loss on Ignition (LOI) test measures the percentage of weight loss in cement when it is heated at high temperatures. This loss occurs due to the evaporation of moisture and the release of carbon dioxide (CO_2), primarily from compounds like free lime and magnesia.

Procedure:

1. Weigh **1.0 g of cement** and place it in a **platinum crucible**.
2. Heat the crucible in a furnace to a temperature of **900°C to 1000°C** for **15 minutes**.
3. After heating, allow the crucible to cool and determine the **loss in weight**.

The loss on ignition should not exceed 5% for all types of cement.

Excessive LOI may indicate poor storage conditions, hydration due to moisture absorption, or improper manufacturing, which can affect the performance of cement in concrete.

CHAPTER 2
AGGREGATES

Introduction

Aggregates provide body to concrete, reduce shrinkage, and contribute to its overall economy. Since aggregates are significantly cheaper than cement, it is economical to use as much aggregate as practically possible. Not only does this reduce the cost, but it also enhances the volume stability of concrete. Aggregates typically constitute 60–70% of the total volume of concrete. However, it is crucial that the aggregates used are strong, as weak aggregates limit the overall strength of the concrete. Hence, the selection of appropriate aggregates becomes vital.

Earlier, aggregates were considered inert materials in concrete. However, it is now understood that their physical, chemical, and thermal properties significantly influence the behavior and performance of concrete.

Types of Aggregates

Based on size, aggregates are broadly classified into two categories:

1. **Fine Aggregate** – Passes through a 4.75 mm sieve.
2. **Coarse Aggregate** – Retained on a 4.75 mm sieve.

Even within each category, aggregates must represent a range of standard sizes as per relevant IS codes. The different sizes are mixed to ensure that the voids created by larger aggregates are filled by the next smaller size. This gradation continues down to the fine aggregate and cement paste, resulting in a compact and dense concrete mass with minimal voids.

Properties of Aggregates

The properties of aggregates can be broadly divided into two categories:

1. Inherited Properties

These are the properties that aggregates acquire from the parent rock:

- Chemical and mineral composition
- Specific gravity
- Hardness
- Strength
- Colour

2. Acquired Properties

These are the properties that aggregates gain during the process of crushing and processing:

- Shape of aggregates
- Size distribution
- Surface texture
- Water absorption

Upon close observation of both categories, it becomes clear that not only the parent rock but also the processing method greatly influences aggregate properties. These acquired characteristics have a significant impact on the behavior of both fresh and hardened concrete. Therefore, thorough evaluation of both inherited and acquired properties is essential before selecting aggregates for concrete.

a. Aggregate Shape

The shape of aggregate particles cannot be defined by exact geometrical figures, but they can be broadly classified into the following types:
(i) Rounded
(ii) Angular
(iii) Elongated
(iv) Flaky
(v) Irregular

The shape of aggregates affects the workability, strength, and durability of concrete. To quantify the shape characteristic, a term called **Angularity Number** is used. It measures the excess percentage of voids in an aggregate sample compared to fully rounded gravel, which typically has 33% voids (or 67% solids).

The formula for Angularity Number is:

$$\text{Angularity Number} = 67 - \left(\frac{\text{Bulk Density}}{\text{Specific Gravity}}\right) \times 100$$

Rounded aggregates have Angularity Number close to 0, while highly angular aggregates may have a number as high as 11.

Flaky aggregates are those with thickness less than 0.6 times the mean sieve size of the fraction they belong to.
Elongated aggregates have a length more than 1.8 times the mean sieve size.
The shape of the aggregate is influenced by the type of crusher used and the reduction ratio. Higher crushing ratios often produce more flaky and elongated particles.
From a practical perspective, rounded aggregates are preferred in low-grade concrete (water-cement ratio > 0.40) due to better workability and reduced cement demand. However, angular aggregates are more suitable for high-strength concrete and pavements where higher interlocking and flexural strength are desired.

Practical Implications

Concrete grade / application	Preferred shape	Reason
Lower-grade concrete (w/c > 0.40)	Rounded	Better workability, lower paste demand
Higher-grade or high-flexure concrete (low w/c)	Angular	Superior interlock, higher aggregate-paste bond strength

b. Aggregate Size

The size of aggregate plays a crucial role in the performance and economy of concrete. **Larger-sized aggregates** are generally preferred due to the following benefits:

1. **Reduction in cement content** – Larger particles reduce the total surface area, requiring less cement paste for coating.
2. **Lower water demand** – Less surface area also means reduced water requirement for lubrication.
3. **Reduced shrinkage** – Less cement paste results in lower drying and plastic shrinkage.

However, the use of larger aggregates is not without limitations. Practical considerations and structural constraints restrict the **Maximum Size of Aggregate (MSA)**, which is governed by the following factors:

- **Thickness of the section:**
  MSA should not exceed **1/4th** of the minimum thickness of the concrete section.
- **Spacing between reinforcement bars:**
  MSA should be at least **5 mm less** than the minimum clear spacing between bars.
- **Clear cover to reinforcement:**
  MSA should also be **5 mm less** than the clear cover provided.

In Plain Concrete (commonly known as Plum Concrete), large-sized rubble or boulders up to 160 mm can be used to economize the mix for mass concreting works.

For Reinforced Cement Concrete (RCC), a 20 mm MSA is standard due to reinforcement spacing and workability concerns.

In Prestressed Concrete (PSC), smaller sizes (generally 10 mm or 12.5 mm) are preferred to ensure better compaction and bonding, especially in dense reinforcement layouts.

c. Surface Texture

Surface texture refers to the degree of roughness or smoothness of the aggregate surface. It significantly affects the **bonding** between the aggregate and the cement paste in concrete. Texture depends on several factors such as:

- **Hardness** of the aggregate
- **Grain size**
- **Pore structure**
- **Exposure to weathering agents** like wind, water, or abrasion

Aggregates can be broadly categorized into two types based on surface texture:

(a) Smooth-Textured Aggregates

These are typically hard, dense, and fine-grained materials. Their surfaces are relatively smooth, offering less surface area for bonding. As a result, they require less paste for lubrication and provide better workability. However, the smooth surface leads to poor mechanical interlock, reducing the bond strength with the cement matrix. Hence, they may deliver higher compressive strength but lower tensile and flexural strength.

(b) Rough-Textured Aggregates

These aggregates have a coarse and irregular surface, offering better mechanical interlocking with the cement paste. They tend to develop higher tensile and flexural strength, but due to their roughness, they require a higher water-cement ratio for the same workability, which may reduce compressive strength.

The influence of texture on concrete strength is shown in the table below:

Smooth (%)	Rough (%)	w/c Ratio	Flexural Strength (MPa)	Compressive Strength (MPa)
100	0	0.54	4.3	34.8
50	50	0.57	4.6	32.1
0	100	0.64	4.8	29.5

d. Water Absorption and Paste Phase in Concrete

In concrete mix design, it is typically assumed that aggregates are in a Saturated Surface Dry (SSD) condition—meaning their pores are full but no moisture is present on the surface. However, aggregates at the site may be in one of the following moisture states:

1. **Bone Dry** – completely dry, with empty pores

2. **Air Dry** – partially saturated, surface dry
3. **SSD (Saturated Surface Dry)** – internal pores filled, surface dry
4. **Moist** – saturated and with surface moisture

If the aggregate is **drier than SSD**, it absorbs water from the mix, reducing workability. If it is **moister than SSD**, it adds unaccounted water, reducing concrete strength. Therefore, proper moisture correction is essential during batching.

Phases of Concrete

Concrete consists of two major phases:

1. **Aggregate Phase** – comprises fine and coarse aggregates
2. **Paste Phase** – made of cement, water, and air voids

Among these, the **paste phase** is typically the weaker component and is often responsible for most durability issues. It has the following characteristics:

- Weaker than aggregates
- More permeable and vulnerable to shrinkage and chemical attacks
- More affected by aggressive environmental conditions

To improve concrete performance and economy, the volume of paste should be minimized. It must be just enough to fill the voids between aggregates and lubricate the mix for proper compaction.

This balance can be achieved through the use of well-graded aggregates, which minimize voids and reduce the required paste content. In turn, this leads to better strength, lower permeability, and improved durability of the concrete.

Sieve Analysis of Aggregates

Sieve analysis is a fundamental method used to determine the particle size distribution, or gradation, of aggregates. In this process, a sample of aggregate is separated into various size fractions using standard sieves. Each fraction consists of particles of similar nominal size.

The standard sieve sizes used for analysis include: 80 mm, 40 mm, 20 mm, 10 mm, 4.75 mm, 2.36 mm, 1.18 mm, 600 μm, 300 μm, and 150 μm.

Gradation plays a critical role in both the strength and workability of concrete. In particular, fine aggregate (FA) gradation significantly affects concrete properties.

- If FA is too coarse, it can lead to segregation, bleeding, and a harsh mix.
- If FA is too fine, it increases the water demand, affecting strength and durability.

To quantify the gradation of FA, a numerical value called the **Fineness Modulus (FM)** is used. It is calculated as:

$$FM = \frac{\text{Cumulative percentage retained on standard sieves}}{100}$$

sieves}}{100}FM=100Cumulative percentage retained on standard sieves

The FM gives an estimate of the average size of the particles. A **larger FM** indicates **coarser sand**, while a **smaller FM** indicates **finer sand**.

Typical FM Ranges for Sand

Sand Type	Fineness Modulus (FM)
Fine Sand	2.2 – 2.6
Medium Sand	2.6 – 2.9
Coarse Sand	2.9 – 3.2

Quality of Aggregates

The quality of aggregates significantly influences the durability and strength of concrete. Aggregates should be clean, durable, and free from harmful substances. Common issues that can deteriorate concrete quality include:

(a) Deleterious Materials

Impurities such as clay, silt, coal, lignite, mica, and shale are termed deleterious. These materials interfere with the hydration process and reduce the bond strength between the aggregate and cement paste. Excessive fine dust or organic matter also affects workability and long-term durability.

(b) Salt Contamination

This problem is prominent with marine or sea-dredged aggregates. The presence of salts like chlorides and sulphates can lead to corrosion of reinforcement and structural deterioration, especially in pre-stressed concrete (PSC) structures.

As per the **Concrete Bridge Code (CBC)**:

- **Chloride limit**:
    - 0.04% by weight of Fine Aggregate (FA)
    - 0.02% by weight of Coarse Aggregate (CA)
- **Sulphate limit**:

- 0.4% by weight of Total Aggregate

Such aggregates should be **thoroughly washed** or **avoided** in critical structural applications.

(c) Alkali-Aggregate Reaction (AAR)

Some aggregates contain reactive silica, which reacts with alkalis in cement (e.g., sodium or potassium oxides) to form an expansive gel. This leads to internal stress, cracking, and long-term deterioration known as Alkali-Silica Reaction (ASR).

To mitigate ASR:

1. Use **Low-Alkali Cement** (alkali content < 0.6%)
2. Add **Pozzolanic materials** (e.g., fly ash or silica fume) to bind the free alkalis before they can attack reactive silica in aggregates.

Gap Grading of Aggregates

Gap grading (or discontinuous grading) departs from the traditional well-graded approach in which all particle sizes are present in suitable proportions. In a well-graded mix, it is assumed that the voids created by larger particles are filled by the next smaller size, and so on, producing maximum density. Field experience, however, shows that the immediate lower size often does not fit into the voids created by a larger size without disturbing the aggregate skeleton—a phenomenon called particle-size interference.

Research indicates that voids formed by a given aggregate size are more effectively filled by particles two or three sizes smaller. For example, cavities created by 40 mm aggregate can readily accept 10 mm or 4.75 mm particles, but not 20 mm. Designing a gradation that deliberately omits one or more intermediate sizes is therefore known as gap grading.

Advantages of Gap-Graded Concrete

1. **Reduced sand requirement** — Fine aggregate content can drop by **25 – 40 %**, lowering cost.
2. **Lower specific surface area** — Fewer fines mean less total surface to coat, thereby cutting **water and cement demand**.
3. **Point-to-point aggregate contact** — The coarse fractions touch at discrete points, which **limits drying shrinkage**.
4. **Cement savings** — With fewer voids to fill, the mix needs **less paste**, enhancing economy and reducing heat of hydration.

Practical Considerations

Gap-graded mixes can be prone to segregation and may not exhibit the expected level of workability. Hence, trial batches and workability tests are essential before full-scale adoption. Proper vibration and control of moisture content are also critical to prevent segregation in the field.

When carefully proportioned and adequately compacted, gap-graded concrete offers an economical route to high strength with lower paste content, particularly in mass concrete and pavement applications.

Bulking of Sand

Bulking refers to the increase in the apparent volume of sand when moisture is present on the surface of its particles. This phenomenon occurs due to the formation of a thin film of water around the sand grains, which leads to the development of surface tension. This tension causes the particles to repel each other, resulting in a loose packing and thereby an increased volume.

Importantly, bulking does not occur when the sand is either completely dry or fully saturated:

- **Dry sand** has no water film, so the particles settle closely without expansion.
- **Saturated sand** loses surface tension as water fills the voids, collapsing the expanded structure.

Key Characteristics:

- **Moisture content** directly affects bulking. The increase in volume is **not linear** but reaches a **maximum** at a certain percentage of moisture (usually around 4–6% by weight).
- **Fineness of sand** influences bulking significantly.
    - **Fine sand** exhibits more bulking than coarse sand.
    - **Very fine sand** can show **up to 38–40% bulking**.

Importance in Concrete Mix Design:

If bulking is not accounted for, it may result in using less sand by weight than required, leading to harsh concrete, poor workability, and inadequate strength. Hence, volume correction is essential when batching by volume, especially in field conditions.

CHAPTER 4

WATER & ADMIXTURE

WATER

Water is a critical ingredient in concrete production, and its quality significantly influences both the strength and durability of the final product. A commonly used rule of thumb is that water suitable for drinking is generally acceptable for making concrete. However, a more technical approach requires compliance with specific chemical and physical standards.

Requirements for Water Quality

- **pH Value**: Should be between **6 and 8**. A pH lower than 6 indicates acidity, which may lead to corrosion of embedded reinforcement.
- **Purity**: The water must be **free from organic matter**, **silt**, **oil**, **sugar**, **chlorides**, and other harmful impurities.

Effects of Water Impurities

1. **Carbonates and Bicarbonates**:
    - These can affect the setting time of cement.
    - Sodium carbonate causes rapid or "flash" setting.
    - If bicarbonate content exceeds 1000 ppm, it is essential to conduct setting time and strength tests before use.
2. **Chlorides and Sulphates (Brackish Water)**:
    - Chloride content should be less than 10,000 ppm.
    - Sulphate content should be less than 3000 ppm.
    - Excessive levels can lead to corrosion and deterioration of concrete.
3. **Turbidity**:
    - Should be below 2000 ppm.
    - High turbidity (due to silt or suspended particles) interferes with setting, hardening, and the bond between cement paste and aggregates.
4. **Algae**:
    - Presence of algae can trap excess water in the mix, reducing the effective water-cement ratio and hence the strength of concrete.

Assessment of Water Quality

When the source of water is uncertain (e.g., coastal or marshy areas), it is advisable to:

- Cast concrete test cubes using both distilled water and available water.
- Compare their compressive strengths at 7 and 28 days.

- If the concrete made with available water achieves at least 90% of the strength of that made with distilled water, and no other adverse effects are observed, the water source may be considered suitable.
- However, such testing should be repeated periodically to ensure continued compliance.

Effect of Sea Water

Sea water contains approximately 3.5% salinity, primarily due to the presence of dissolved chlorides, sulphates, and other salts. While it may seem convenient to use sea water in coastal regions, its use in concrete presents several serious concerns:

Key Adverse Effects of Sea Water on Concrete

1. **Corrosion of Reinforcement**
   The chlorides in sea water are highly corrosive to steel. When used in reinforced concrete, sea water accelerates the corrosion of embedded steel bars, leading to structural deterioration, cracking, and loss of durability over time.
2. **Reduction in Strength**
   The use of sea water in concrete leads to a strength reduction of about 10–15%, depending on the salt concentration and type of cement used.
3. **Accelerated Setting Time**
   Sea water tends to speed up the setting of cement, which may affect the workability and finishing operations during concrete placement.
4. **Efflorescence**
   The presence of soluble salts can cause efflorescence—the white, powdery deposit often seen on the surface of concrete due to salt migration and crystallization.
5. **Persistent Dampness**
   Salt retention in concrete can lead to continuous moisture retention, causing damp surfaces and reducing the material's aesthetic and functional performance.

ADMIXTURE

Admixtures are optional ingredients in concrete that are added in small quantities to modify the properties of both fresh and hardened concrete or grout materials to meet specific performance requirements. They are used to alter workability, setting time, strength development, durability, permeability, and appearance, depending on the application.

Although admixtures are not mandatory in all concrete mixes, the use of chemical admixtures becomes essential when producing high-performance or high-grade concrete.

Categories of Admixtures

Concrete admixtures are classified based on their function. The major categories are:

1. **Water-Reducing Admixtures**
2. **Retarding Admixtures**
3. **Air-Entraining Admixtures**
4. **Accelerating Admixtures**

1. Water-Reducing Admixtures

These admixtures reduce the amount of water required to achieve a desired workability. While the theoretical water-cement (w/c) ratio for complete hydration is around 0.23, much higher values (typically 0.4–0.6) are used in practice to ensure proper mixing, transportation, placing, and compaction.

Workability is critical in concrete design, as inadequate workability leads to honeycombing, segregation, and non-uniform strength distribution. Water-reducing admixtures help achieve the needed workability without increasing the water content unnecessarily.

Types of Water Reducers

(a) Plasticizers
Also known as normal water reducers, these can reduce the water demand by up to 15%.

(b) Superplasticizers
Also known as High-Range Water Reducers (HRWR), they can reduce water demand by 20–30% or more. These are enhanced formulations of plasticizers, used in high-performance concrete.

Mechanism of Water Reduction

Water-reducing admixtures act as surface-active agents (surfactants). In a normal mix, cement particles, due to their fine size and electrical properties, tend to flocculate (cluster together), trapping a significant amount of water within the flocs. This entrapped water does not contribute to workability.

When water-reducing admixtures are added:

- They induce negative charges on the surfaces of cement particles.
- This causes electrostatic repulsion between the flocculated particles.
- The cement particles become dispersed, releasing the entrapped water.
- As a result, more water becomes available for workability, even though the total water content is reduced.

This action enhances **workability, strength**, and **durability**, without increasing water content.

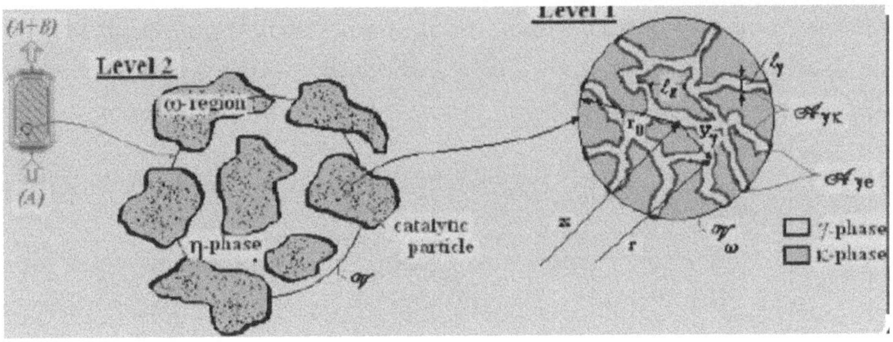

Physical Interaction of Super-Plasticizer

2. Retarding Admixtures

Retarding admixtures are used in concrete where a delay in the setting time is required. These admixtures slow down the rate of hydration of cement, thereby extending the initial setting time without affecting the ultimate strength or long-term hydration process.

Purpose and Applications

- Retarders are particularly useful in hot weather concreting, where high temperatures accelerate setting, making proper placement and compaction difficult.
- They help to prevent cold joints, which occur when fresh concrete is placed over partially set concrete.
- They are also beneficial in mass concrete works, long-distance transportation of concrete, or large pours, where delays between successive batches are expected.

Key Characteristics

- Retarding admixtures can extend the initial setting time by 3 hours or more, depending on the dosage and environmental conditions.
- The final strength and durability of concrete remain largely unaffected.
- They provide sufficient time for mixing, placing, vibrating, and finishing, especially in complex or large pours.

3. Air-Entraining Admixtures

Air-entraining admixtures are surface-active agents added to concrete to introduce and stabilize microscopic air bubbles, typically ranging in size from 5 μm to 80 μm. These air voids are evenly distributed throughout the concrete and remain stable during mixing, placing, and setting.

Mechanism of Action

- These admixtures function by reducing surface tension, allowing stable air bubbles to be incorporated during mixing.
- The air bubbles break the capillary structure of hardened concrete, thereby reducing permeability and increasing durability.

- They also act like tiny ball bearings in the mix, improving mobility and cohesion of the ingredients, which enhances workability without the need for additional water.

Benefits of Air-Entraining Admixtures

- **Improved Workability**: Makes the mix more cohesive and easier to place, especially in lean or harsh mixes.
- **Enhanced Resistance to Freeze-Thaw Cycles**: The entrained air voids provide space for water to expand when it freezes, thereby preventing cracking and surface scaling in cold climates.
- **Reduced Bleeding and Segregation**: Helps to stabilize the mix by minimizing movement of water and aggregates.
- **Increased Durability**: Lowers the permeability of concrete and protects against sulfate attack and weathering.

4. Accelerating Admixtures

Accelerating admixtures shorten the setting time and speed up the early-age strength development of concrete.
They are indispensable when concrete must reach serviceability quickly, such as:

- Concreting in flowing or tidal water, where early stiffening resists wash-out.
- Cold-weather concreting, to offset slow hydration at low temperatures.
- Rapid road or runway repairs and precast operations, where early demoulding or load application is critical.

Super-Plasticizers: The Workhorse of High-Performance Concrete

Among all admixtures, water-reducing agents—especially super-plasticizers—are used most frequently in modern high-performance concrete. Four principal families are common in practice:

Code	Chemical Base	Typical Climate Suitability	Key Strength
(a)	**Sulphonated Melamine Formaldehyde (SMF)**	Cool or cold regions	Gives very rapid early strength gain; useful for precast work in winter.
(b)	**Sulphonated Naphthalene Formaldehyde (SNF)**	Hot climates	Maintains dispersion efficiency at elevated temperatures; good slump retention in heat.

(c)	**Modified Lignosulphonates**	Wide temperature swings (typical Indian conditions)	Economical, moderate water reduction, compatible with most cements.
(d)	**Poly-Carboxylate Ethers (PCE)**	Whenever long workability retention is needed	Highest water reduction (25 – 35 %), excellent slump retention without set delay.

Factors Influencing Admixture Performance

1. **Chemical Type & Molecular Weight**
   - Higher-molecular-weight super-plasticizers generally provide stronger electrostatic and steric dispersion, hence greater water reduction.
2. **Dosage (Optimum Proportioning)**
   - Underdosing ⇒ insufficient effect
   - Overdosing ⇒ segregation, bleeding, excessive retardation, or rapid slump loss (depending on type)
   - Determine the optimum by laboratory trial mixes under site-simulated conditions.
3. **Cement Chemistry & Fineness**
   - High C_3A content or very fine cements may demand higher dosages or different admixture chemistry.
4. **Water Chemistry**
   - Chloride, sulphate, or high alkalinity in mixing water can alter admixture efficiency.
5. **Temperature & Time**
   - Heat accelerates most reactions; cold slows them. Choose admixture type and dosage accordingly.
6. **Presence of Supplementary Cementitious Materials**
   - Fly ash, slag, silica fume, and metakaolin each interact differently; re-optimise dosage when SCM proportions change.

With these four classes and influencing factors clearly understood, you can tailor admixture selection and proportions to meet virtually any performance requirement—whether it is extended workability, rapid turnaround, or enhanced durability.

Recommended Methods for Better Performance of Admixtures

To ensure optimal performance of admixtures—particularly super-plasticizers—it is essential to follow proper mixing and handling techniques. The effectiveness of admixtures depends not only on their type and dosage but also on the method of incorporation into the concrete mix.

Recommended Procedure

(a) Add all aggregates, cement, and approximately 2 litres less than the total required mixing water into the mixer. Mix thoroughly for at least 2 minutes to ensure even distribution.

(b) Dissolve the admixture in the remaining water (2 litres), and then add this solution to the mix. Continue mixing for at least 1 more minute to allow uniform dispersion of the admixture.

(c) When using a transit mixer for Ready Mix Concrete (RMC), the plasticizer should be added just a few minutes before loading to preserve slump and maintain high workability during transport.

(d) For extended operations, it is preferable to add plasticizer in small dosages at regular intervals rather than a single large dose. This improves slump retention and enhances dispersion.

(e) In some cases, an initial overdose of plasticizer may be used to attain high initial workability, followed by a supplementary dosage just before placement to regain workability if lost.

Table–1: Effect of Super-Plasticizer on Workability and Strength

A – Effect on Workability (Water–Cement Ratio Constant)

Mix	Cement (kg/m^3)	w/c	Slump (mm)	Strength (N/mm^2) 7 Days	Strength (N/mm^2) 28 Days
Cement only	440	0.37	25	39.0	54.0
Cement + 0.4% Admixture	440	0.37	100	41.1	54.1

Observation: At the same water–cement ratio, the use of 0.4% super-plasticizer significantly improved workability (from 25 mm to 100 mm slump) with no loss in strength.

B – Effect on Strength (Workability Constant)

Mix	Cement (kg/m³)	w/c	Slump (mm)	Strength (N/mm²) 7 Days	Strength (N/mm²) 28 Days
Cement only	315	0.60	95	21.8	29.1
Cement + 0.4% Admixture	315	0.53	95	28.5	37.5

Observation: To maintain the same slump (95 mm), the addition of 0.4% admixture allowed for a reduction in w/c ratio from 0.60 to 0.53, leading to a substantial increase in compressive strength.

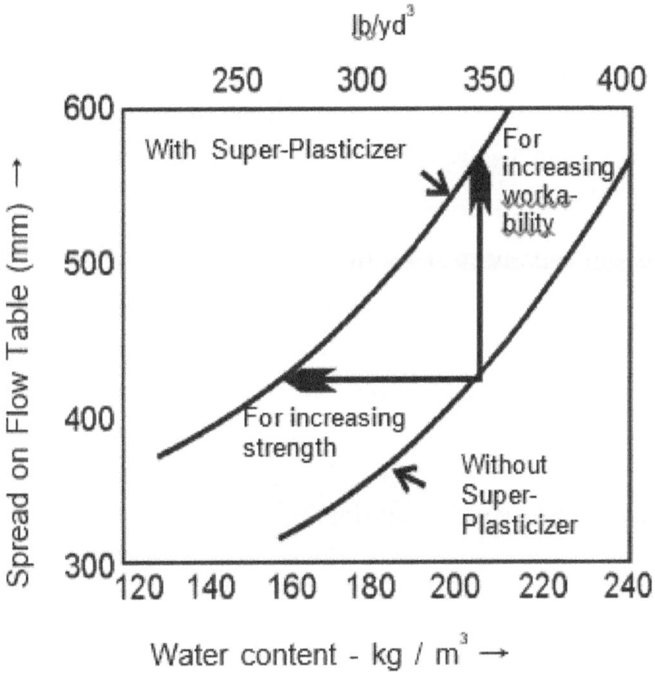

Effect of Super-Plasticizer

CHAPTER 5

MIX DESIGN

Definition of Mix Design

Mix design is the process of selecting appropriate ingredients of concrete—such as cement, water, fine and coarse aggregates, and admixtures—and determining their relative proportions to achieve the desired properties in the most economical way. The main objective is to produce concrete that meets the required levels of workability, strength, durability, and performance under specific conditions, while minimizing cost and wastage.

A well-designed concrete mix should be workable enough for proper placement and compaction, strong enough to bear the anticipated loads, durable enough to withstand environmental exposure, and economical enough for practical use. Achieving this balance involves a deep understanding of the physical and chemical properties of each ingredient, such as the grading of aggregates, the setting time and fineness of cement, the water-cement ratio, and the impact of chemical or mineral admixtures.

However, mix design is not merely a theoretical process. It requires significant experience and judgment. Much like cooking, where a perfect recipe alone does not guarantee a delicious meal without the skill of the cook, good quality concrete cannot be produced without the knowledge and practical experience of a concrete technologist or site engineer. Field trials, adjustments, and feedback are essential parts of successful mix design. Thus, mix design is both a science and an art, combining technical specifications with field experience to produce concrete that performs effectively and efficiently in real-world conditions.

Types of Mix Design

Concrete mix design can be broadly classified into two main categories:

1. **Nominal Mix**
2. **Design Mix**

1. Nominal Mix

Nominal mix is a simplified method of concrete mix proportioning, generally used for small-scale or less critical construction works where exact strength and durability requirements are not very stringent. In this method, the proportions of the ingredients are pre-fixed by standard codes (such as IS 456:2000), based on past experience and established practice.

For example, a nominal mix of M15 concrete typically uses a cement:sand:coarse aggregate ratio of 1:2:4 by volume. These fixed proportions are easy to use on site and do not require sophisticated testing or equipment.

Nominal mixes are recommended for concrete of M20 grade or lower. While they offer simplicity and convenience, they do not account for the variability in material properties (such as moisture content, aggregate grading, etc.), and may result in overuse of cement, making them less economical and potentially inconsistent in performance.

The various ingredients are taken as given below in **Table**.

Table-1: Nominal Mix Proportions for Different Grades of Concrete

Grade of Concrete	Max. Quantity of Dry Aggregates per 50 kg of Cement (kg)	FA:CA Ratio (by mass)	Max. Quantity of Water (litres)
M-5	800	Generally 1:2 (may vary from 1:1.5 to 1:2.5)	60
M-7.5	625	—	45
M-10	480	—	34
M-15	330	—	32
M-20	250	—	30

2. Design Mix

Design Mix refers to a performance-based approach to concrete mix design. In this method, the selection and proportioning of ingredients are done by the designer, based on the desired performance characteristics. The user only needs to specify the **requirements** of the concrete in:

- **Fresh state:** Workability and finishing characteristics.
- **Hardened state:** Primarily compressive strength and durability.

Designation of Concrete

Concrete is generally designated based on its compressive strength, known as the Grade of Concrete.
According to IS 456:2000, the grade of concrete is defined as the characteristic compressive strength of a 15 cm concrete cube after 28 days, expressed in N/mm² (MPa).

For example:

- M20 grade concrete has a characteristic compressive strength of **20 N/mm²** at 28 days.

Sampling of Concrete

Sampling of concrete is an essential part of quality control and ensures that the concrete used in construction meets the required specifications.

1. Number of Samples Required

The number of concrete samples to be taken depends on the **quantity of concrete** placed on a particular day, as shown in **Table-2** below:

Table-2: Number of Samples Based on Quantity of Concrete

Quantity of Concrete (m^3)	Number of Samples
1 – 5	1
6 – 15	2
16 – 30	3
31 – 50	4
51 & above	4 + 1 additional sample for each 50 m^3 or part thereof

Cube Casting

Cube specimens are cast using the **same concrete** that is being placed in the structure to ensure accurate representation of strength.

Procedure:

1. **Filling the Mould:**
    - Concrete is filled into the cube mould in **three equal layers**.
    - Each layer is **compacted** using a **bullet-headed tamping rod**:
        - **Rod Specifications**: 16 mm diameter, 600 mm length.
        - **Number of Strokes**: 35 strokes per layer, uniformly distributed.
2. **Alternative Compaction Method (Using Needle Vibrator):**
    - Do **not insert** the needle vibrator directly into the cube mould.
    - Instead, place a **wooden piece** over the cube mould and apply vibration by touching the needle **at the center** of the wooden piece.
    - This ensures **indirect vibration** and prevents segregation or over-compaction.
3. **Marking:**
    - Lightly mark the **date and cube number** on the surface of the fresh concrete ("green concrete") for identification.
4. **Initial Curing:**
    - Cover the mould with a **damp cloth** to prevent moisture loss.
5. **De-moulding:**
    - The cube is **removed from the mould** after **16 to 24 hours**.

6. **Final Curing:**
    - After de-moulding, the cube is **submerged in a clean water tank or curing pond** until the day of testing (typically 7 or 28 days).

Cube Testing

Testing Procedure:

- **Sample Definition**:
  One sample of concrete comprises three cubes of size 150 mm × 150 mm × 150 mm.
- **Acceptability Criteria**:
  The individual strength of any of the three cubes should not vary by more than ±15% from the average strength of the three cubes.
  If the variation exceeds this limit, the sample is considered invalid.
- **Positioning During Test**:
  While testing, place the cube in the compression testing machine such that the smooth cast faces (those in contact with mould) are kept at the top and bottom.
- **Rate of Loading**:
  The **loading rate** should not exceed **14 N/mm² per minute**.
  Higher loading rates may give **inaccurate or misleading results.**

Importance of Cube Test

While cube strength does not exactly represent the strength of concrete in the structure, it is still widely used due to the following reasons:

1. **Indicates Potential Strength**
   It provides an estimate of the maximum possible strength of the concrete mix under ideal conditions.
2. **Detects Quality Control Issues**
   It helps identify inconsistencies in batching, mixing, and materials at the site.
3. **Monitors Strength Development**
   By testing cubes at various ages (e.g., 7 days, 28 days), we can observe the rate of strength gain.
4. **Assists in Formwork Removal Decisions**
   Cube strength guides the decision for **safe removal of formwork**, especially in early stages.

Limitations of Cube Strength

Despite its importance, cube strength does not directly reflect the actual strength of concrete in the structure due to several reasons:

1. **Ideal vs. Real Conditions**
    - Concrete in the cube does **not undergo** the same **handling processes** as structural concrete:
        - Transportation
        - Placement

        - Compaction
        - Curing
    - These processes are generally **more carefully controlled** for cube samples.
2. **Shape Factor Effect**
    - Cubes are **uniform in shape**, whereas concrete in structures has **varied shapes and stress distributions**.
    - Because of this, **actual structural strength** is typically **around two-thirds** of the cube strength for the same concrete mix.

Statistical Interpretation of Cube Results

Why Statistical Analysis is Needed

The **compressive strength of concrete cubes** is influenced by several factors, including:

- Quality and proportion of materials
- Mixing method
- Compaction
- Curing conditions
- Testing procedure

Even when all these factors are kept constant, cube strength values from the same batch can still vary. This natural variation makes it essential to use statistical tools for interpreting test results, especially when evaluating compliance with specifications.

Normal Distribution of Results

When a **large number of cube strength values**, obtained under similar conditions, are plotted on a **histogram**, the distribution typically follows a **bell-shaped curve**, known as a **Normal Distribution Curve**.

Key Characteristics of Normal Distribution:

- The **peak of the curve** represents the **mean (average)** strength.
- Most of the test results lie **close to the mean**.
- As we move away from the mean (higher or lower), the **frequency of values decreases**.
- The **spread of the curve** indicates the level of **quality control**.

Interpretation of Curve Spread (Quality Control)

A graphical representation (Fig-1) often shows **three typical curves**, representing different levels of quality control:

Curve	Interpretation	Remarks
Curve 1	Very Good Quality Control	Very narrow spread; results closely packed around the mean
Curve 2	Good Quality Control	Moderate spread; acceptable variation

Curve 3	Poor Quality Control	Wide spread; large variability in results

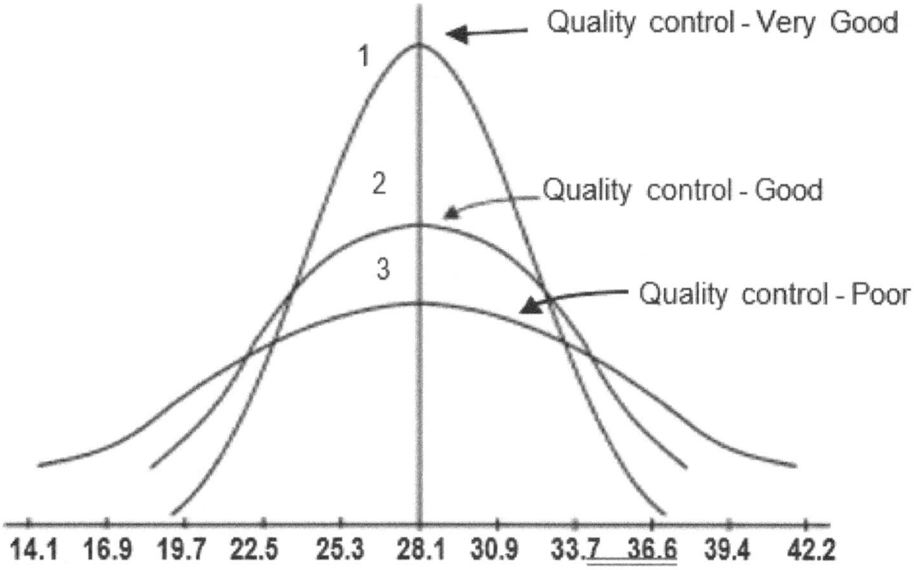

Statistically this deviation is known as **'Standard Deviation'** and it can be calculated by the formula given below.

$$S.D.\ (\sigma) = \sqrt{\frac{\sum (x-\mu)^2}{n-1}}$$

Where x = value for individual cube

n = total number of cubes.

μ = Arithemetic mean of 'n' cubes

S.D. will be less if the 'Quality Control' at site is better and most of the cube results will be clustered near the mean value. If quality control is poor, the test results will have value much different from mean value and therefore, Standard Deviation will be higher.

Target Mean Strength

From the behaviour of the 'Normal Distribution Curve', it is clear that when we are testing a large number of cubes, all the cubes will not have the same strength even if these are cast and tested in identical conditions. Some cubes will have higher strength than mean value whereas other cubes will have lower strength. The deviation from the mean value is indicated by 'Standard Deviation'. It has been found from the experiments that the area under the 'Normal Distribution

Curve' will follow certain behaviour such that the area covered within a distance equal to one S.D. on either side from mean will be equal to 34.1% of total area. Simi- larly second and third S.D. on each side will cover additional area of 13.6% and 2.2% respectively. Combined together, approximately 99.9% area will be covered within distance equal to 3 x S.D. on each side from mean value as shown in **Fig-2**.

From this figure it is also clear that if we require the strength equal to mean value, probability is that only 50% cubes will have strength equal to or more than the required strength. If we want to increase the percentage of cubes

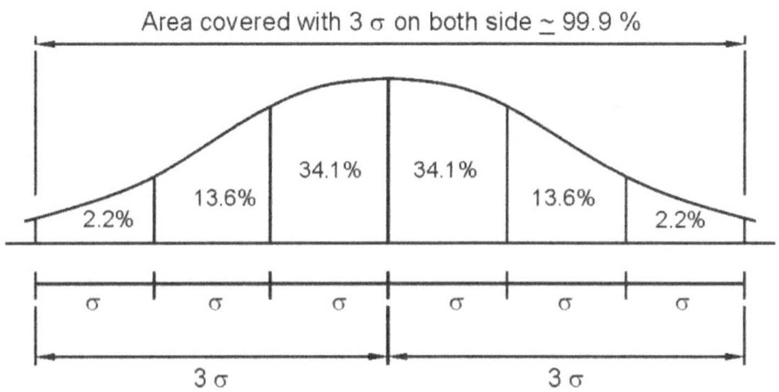

Fig-2

having strength equal or more than the required strength, we will have to target for higher strength. So instead of plac- ing the desired strength at mean value, place it on the left side of mean value by a distance equal to k x S.D. where k will depend upon the percentage of cubes we want to have strength equal or more than the desired strength. This is depicted in **Fig-3**

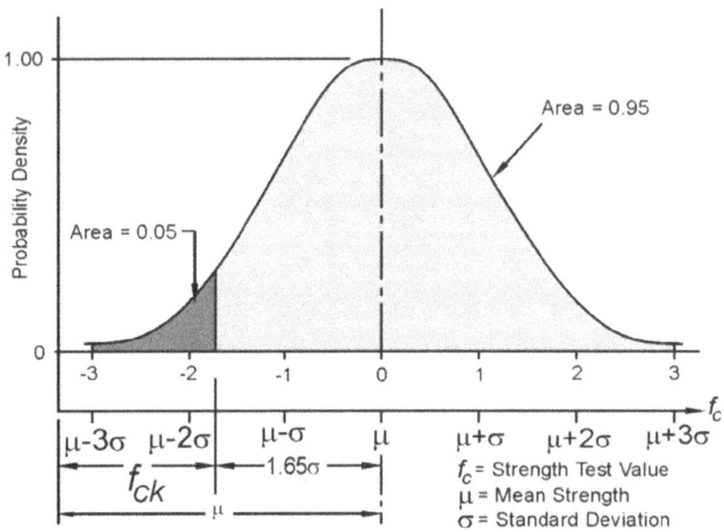

Fig-3

As per IS : 456:2000, this percentage is 95% and therefore the desired strength has to be placed it 1.65 times

S.D. left of mean, such that now

mean = desired strength + 1.65 x S.D.

In fact, the desired strength is called 'Characteristic Strength' and the mean value is called 'Target Mean Strength'. Therefore,

TMS = fck + 1.65 x S.D.

The value of 1.65 is based upon the provision that 5% of the test results can be accepted having lower than the required strength.

Understanding of Normal Distribution Curve

The ordinate, 'Probability Density' as given in **Fig-3** is often misunderstood. It doesn't represent the number of cubes at a particular strength. In fact, it shows the probabil- ity of concentration of test results at this strength as shown in **Fig-4.**

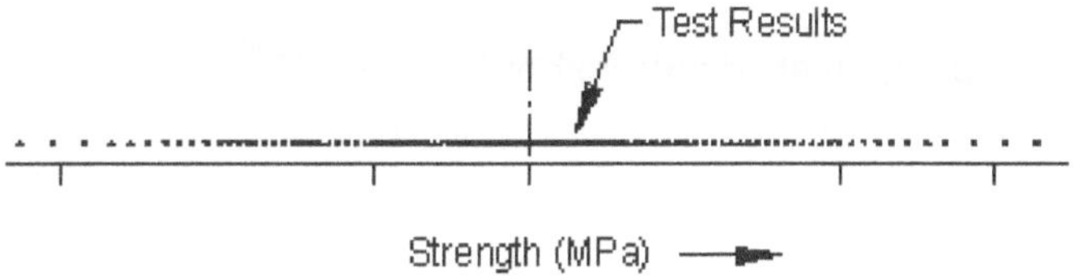

Fig-4 Probability Density of cube results

The concentration at mean value depends upon 'quality control' and S.D. If value of S.D. is less, the prob- ability of concentration of test results will be higher at the mean value and therefore, the curve will shrink from both side and rise at centre as shown by 'curve 1' in **Fig-1.**

Acceptance Criteria (As per IS-456:2000)

While designing the mix, we have to target for a higher strength called 'Target Mean Strength' so that not more than 5% test results fall below a desired strength called 'fck' i.e. Characteristics Strength (CS).

When we test a large number of cubes, a few cubes will certainly have strength below CS. This is perfectly in accordance with the design criteria of mix. Therefore, we should not worry if some of the cubes have less strength than CS. We should also not attempt to manipulate the test results. As per IS-456:2000, there is a well-defined criteria for acceptance of compressive strength of cubes. The test result will be accepted when the following two criteria are satisfied.

The mean strength determined from any group of four consecutive test results should comply with the following condition:

For M-15

Mean ≥ fck + 0.825 x S.D.

or

≥ fck + 3 N/mm^2 whichever is greater.

For M-20 & above

Mean ≥ fck + 0.825 x S. D.
or
≥ fck + 4 N/mm^2 whichever is greater.

Any individual test result should not have value less than fck - 3 N/mm^2 for M-15 and fck - 4 N/mm^2 for M-20 and above.

Note : In above criteria, S.D. should be established at site after obtaining the test results of a minimum 30 samples.

Acceptance criteria (As per CBC)

In CBC, the values are for M-20 and above only.
The two criterion are as given below :
The mean of 4 consecutive test results should exceed 'fck' by at least 3 N/mm^2.
Any individual test result should not be less than 'fck' by 3 N/mm^2.

Aim of Mix Design :

Before attempting to design a mix with the above requirements i.e. strength and workability, we should be clear about what we are going to do. It is not simply a series of calculations for obtaining the quantities of various materials i.e. cement, sand, coarse aggregates and water. In fact it is much more than that. Mix design means obtaining our own curve representing the relationship between strength and water-cement ratio.
We know the trend of the curve. The strength will reduce with increase in water-cement ratio. But we want the exact relationship corresponding to the actual material used at site and actual workmanship achieved at site. Thus the entire exercise of designing a mix is the process of obtaining our own curve between strength and water-cement ratio and then specifying the proportions of all the ingredients.
Step-1 Target Mean Strength

$$TMS = fck + 1.65 \times \text{Standard Deviation (S.D.)}$$

where
fck = Characteristic strength of concrete

SD depends upon grade of concrete and 'Quality Control' of concrete. The assumed S.D. as per IS : 10262- 1982 are given in Table-3.

Table-3

Grade of Concrete	Assumed S.D. Value in N/mm^2
M-10 &15	3.5
M-20 & 25	4.0
M-30 to 55	5.0

In our problem, the concrete grade is M-20. Therefore the value of S.D. is 4.0.

Therefore, TMS = 20 + 1.65 x 4.0

= 26.60 N/mm^2 or 27 N/mm^2

Step- 2 Water–Cement Ratio

A graph between 28 days compressive strength in N/mm^2 and w/c ratio is available for different grades of cement. In graph there are 6 curves, A to F, depending upon 28 days strength of cement. Curve A is at bottom showing less strength of cement and Curve F is at the top representing highest strength of cement. Therefore, before using this graph, we have to find the actual 28 days strength of cement and then identify the curve to be used depending upon this strength.

Let us assume curve 'C' belongs to cement used in our Mix. For curve 'C', the value of w/c ratio obtained from the graph is 0.47 corresponding to TMS = 27 N/mm^2.

This w/c ratio shall be compared with the maximum w/c ratio permissible from the durability consideration. For bridge construction, we can refer Para 5.4.3 of 'Concrete Bridge Code'. From this consideration, the value of maximum w/c ratio for RCC construction and 'Moderate' exposure condition is 0.45. Therefore, we adopt the lower of two i.e. 0.45.

Step- 3 Estimation of air in concrete

The entrapped air in concrete depends on nominal size of aggregate. More air is entrapped in smaller size aggregates as compared to larger size as given below in **Table-4**

Table-4

Nominal Maximum Size of Aggregates	Entrapped Air (% volume of concrete)
10 mm	3%
20 mm	**2%**
40 mm	1%

In our problem, for 20 mm size of aggregate, the entrapped air will be 2%. Step- 4 Estimation of water and sand in concrete

The quantity of water and sand in concrete depends upon MSA and Grade of concrete. Less water is required for higher grade of concrete and higher size of aggregates. The values as per IS : 10262 – 2009 are given in **Table-5**.

Table-5

MSA (mm)		Quantity of water for each m^3 of concrete	Percentage of coarse aggregateby volume of total aggregates			
		Zone	IV	III	II	I
10		208	50	48	46	44
20		186	66	64	62	60
40		165	75	73	71	69

For our problem, MSA = 20 mm and Grade of Concrete = M-20

Therefore, quantity of water = 186 kg per m^3 of concrete.

$$p = \frac{\text{Volume of sand}}{\text{Total volume of aggregate}} = 1-0.6=0.4 \text{ (for zone I)}$$

But the values given in the above table are based on the following assumptions :

Workability of concrete is 25 to 50mm slump.
w/c ratio is 0.50.
Angular aggregates are used.

When the above conditions regarding workability, w/c ratio, fine aggregates etc. are not fulfilled, then certain adjustments need to be made in water content and percentage of sand. These adjustments will be as given in **Table-6**.

Table-6

Change in condition	Adjustment in	
	Water content	% age of sand in total aggregates
Increase/decrease of workability by each 25mm from 25 to 50mm slump	± 3%	NIL
Each 0.05 increase or decrease in water cement ratio w.r.t. 0.50.	NIL	± 1%
For rounded aggregates	-25 kg/cm^3	- 7%

In our problem, the following adjustment will be made as given in **Table-7**.

Table-7

Conditions in our problem	Adjustment in	
	Water content	**% age of sand in total aggregates**
Workability 25 to 50 mm slump.	NIL	NIL
Decrease in water content 0.5 – 0.45 = 0.05	NIL	-0.05/0.05 = -1 %
Angular aggregates	NIL	NIL
Total	NIL	- 1%

Final value of water content = 186 kg Final Value of p = 40 – 1 = 39%
Step-5 Calculation of cement quantity

C = w/(w/c) = 186/0.45 = 413 kg

This quantity of cement needs to be checked against requirement from durability consideration.

From Concrete Bridge Code for RCC structure (Moderate exposure) :
Min. cement = 300 kg Max. cement = 500 kg

Hence the calculated value of C = 413 kg is adopted.

Step-6 Calculation of Aggregate content

We have already calculated water and cement for one cubic meter of concrete. Since the ratio of fine to total aggregate is already determined, the total aggregate content per unit volume of concrete can be calculated from the equation given below :

Gross vol. of conc. = Volume of water + volume of cement
+ volume of total aggregates
+ volume of entrapped air in concrete

Net volume (V) = Volume of water + volume of cement
+ volume of total aggregates

$$p = \frac{\text{Volume of fine aggregate}}{\text{Volume of total aggregate}}$$

or

Volume of total aggregate = 1/p x volume of fine aggregate Therefore,

V = (Wt of water/sp. gr. of water) + (Wt of cement/sp. gr. of cement) + 1/p x volume of fine aggregate

or

$$V = \frac{W}{1} + \frac{C}{Sc} + \frac{1}{p}$$ (wt. of fine aggregate/sp.gr.of fine aggregate)

$$V = \frac{W}{1} + \frac{C}{Sc} + \frac{1}{p}\frac{FA}{Sfa} \quad \ldots\ldots\ldots\ldots\ldots\ldots\ldots\ldots\ldots\ldots\ldots (1)$$

In this equation, we know all the variables except FA, i.e. total weight of fine aggregate per m^3 of concrete.

$$0.98 \times 1000 = \frac{186}{1.0} + \frac{413}{3.15} + \frac{FA}{0.39 \times 2.7}$$

∴ Wt. of fine aggregate FA = 698 kg Similarly using the equation

for CA

$$V = W + \frac{C}{Sc} + \left(\frac{1}{1-p}\right)\frac{CA}{Sca} \quad \ldots\ldots\ldots\ldots\ldots\ldots\ldots\ldots\ldots\ldots\ldots (2)$$

$$0.98 \times 1000 = \frac{186}{1.0} + \frac{413}{3.15} + \left(\frac{1}{1-0.39}\right) \times \frac{CA}{2.5}$$

Wt. of coarse aggregate CA = 1011 kg

Therefore, the values obtained per cubic metre of concrete so far are as given under:

Cement = 413 kg
Water content = 186 kg Fine aggregate = 698 kg
Coarse aggregate = 1011 kg

Step-7 Trial Mixes

Prepare the concrete mix with the above proportion of ingredients and find out the workability. Let us call this trial mix as **TM-0**. If the workability is exactly same as required i.e. 25 to 50mm slump, then no further adjustment is made. But if the measured workability is different from initially assumed, then water content adjustment will again be made accordingly to **Table-6**. Keeping the water cement ratio same, the quantity of cement will also be adjusted. Now the final quantities of other materials will again be calculated using the equations (1) and (2) as the water and cement quantities have changed now. Let us call this trial mix as **TM-1**.

Two more trial mixes **TM-2 & TM-3** will be made, one with 10% less w/c and other with 10% more w/c but keeping the water content same. All these trial mixes are shown in **Table-8.**

Table-8

	Water (kg)	**Cement (kg)**	**w/c**	**FA (kg)**	**CA (kg)**
TM-0	W=186	C=413	0.45	698	1011
TM-1	W1	C1	0.45	FA1	CA1
TM-2	W1	C2	0.9x0.45	FA2	CA2
TM-3	W1	C3	1.1x0.45	FA3	CA3

Now we will cast one sample (three cubes) with each trial mix and find out the 28 days' compressive strength. This strength is plotted against w/c ratio and a curve will be obtained as given under in **Fig-4**.

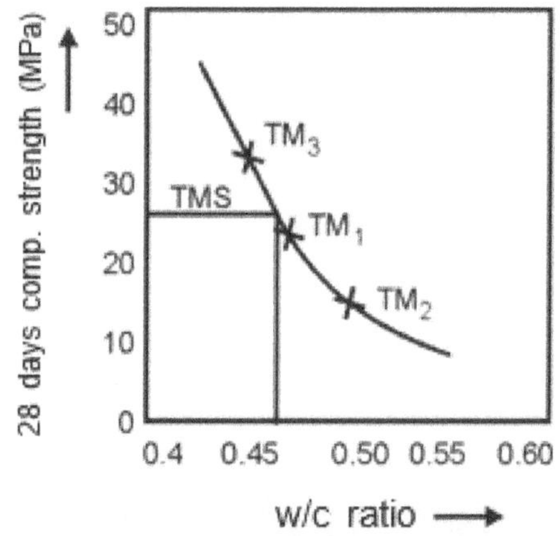

Fig-4 Strength v/s w/c ratio

From the above curve we can determine the w/c for the required TMS of our design mix. This w/c is used to calculate again the ingredient quantities using equation (1) and (2), so that the mix prepared with these quantities will satisfy the requirements of not only strength but workability also. This entire process is nothing but the mix-design.

CHAPTER 6

SPECIAL CONCRETE

LIGHTWEIGHT CONCRETE

Lightweight concrete is a category of concrete that incorporates materials or techniques aimed at reducing its overall density. It often contains an expanding agent or lightweight aggregates that enhance volume and provide advantages such as improved workability and reduced dead load. Compared to conventional concrete, it is significantly lighter, making it particularly useful for structural applications where weight reduction is critical.

Although the unit cost of lightweight concrete materials may be higher than that of traditional concrete, this cost is generally offset by reductions in the total volume of concrete required and the amount of reinforcement steel needed. These savings result from the decreased structural load the concrete imposes.

Advantages of Lightweight Concrete:

- Significant reduction in dead load, leading to savings in foundation size and reinforcement requirements.
- Enhanced thermal insulation properties.
- Better resistance to fire.
- Easier and more cost-effective transportation and handling of precast elements.
- Reduced demand for formwork and temporary supports during construction.

Limitations:

- Highly sensitive to the water content in the mix; even slight variations can impact performance.
- Placement and finishing can be challenging due to the porous and angular nature of lightweight aggregates.
- Requires longer mixing time to ensure a uniform and cohesive mix.

Lightweight Aggregate Concrete

This type of concrete uses specially manufactured or naturally occurring lightweight aggregates in place of regular coarse aggregates. These aggregates, often expanded clay, shale, or slate, reduce the overall density of the concrete while maintaining adequate strength and durability for structural applications. It is commonly used in the production of concrete blocks, structural components, and pavement layers.

Foam Concrete (Lightweight Cellular Concrete)

Foam concrete, also referred to as Lightweight Cellular Concrete (LCC) or Low-Density Cellular Concrete (LDCC), is a type of concrete that incorporates a significant amount of air bubbles into a cement slurry. This is achieved by introducing pre-formed foam into the mix, typically accounting for at least 20% of the volume.

This form of concrete typically exhibits:

- A 28-day compressive strength of around 17 MPa (2500 psi).
- A dry density ranging from 1120 to 1920 kg/m³ (70 to 120 lb/ft³).
- A composition that may include either all lightweight aggregates or a mix of lightweight and normal-density aggregates.

Foam concrete is particularly suitable for non-structural applications, thermal insulation, and situations where reduced weight is essential.

CELLULAR CONCRETE

Cellular concrete is a lightweight, cement-based construction material that contains uniformly distributed air voids throughout its volume. These air pockets are formed using either chemical reactions (gas concrete) or by mixing pre-formed foam into a cementitious slurry (foam concrete). The result is a low-density material with improved insulation properties and reduced weight, making it ideal for various building and infrastructure applications.

This type of concrete is commonly used in:

- Roof and floor decking systems
- Void filling and slip-lining in geotechnical works
- Architectural precast units
- Insulating fills for trench backfills and abandoned pipe lines

Materials Used in Cellular Concrete

1. **Cement**
   The primary binder used in cellular concrete may include Ordinary Portland Cement, cement-silica mixtures, cement-pozzolana combinations, or lime-based binders. These create a uniform paste in which the cellular structure is maintained.

2. **FlyAsh**
   Fly ash, a by-product of coal combustion, is frequently used as a partial cement replacement. It improves workability, reduces the weight of the concrete, and provides an environmentally sustainable solution for industrial waste disposal.

3. **FoamingAgent**
   The foam used in cellular concrete is generated from organic compounds such as Genfil. Bubble sizes typically range from 0.1 mm to 1.5 mm in diameter. The foam is produced with the help of a foam generator and ensures an even distribution of air voids within the mix.

Relevant Standards

The following ASTM standards govern the materials and properties of cellular concrete:

- **ASTM C869** – Specification for foaming agents used in making preformed foam for cellular concrete.
- **ASTM C796** – Test method for evaluating foaming agents in preformed foam production.
- **ASTM C495** – Method for testing compressive strength of lightweight insulating concrete.

Types of Cellular Concrete (Based on Density)

Cellular concrete is classified into three types depending on its density and application:

1 High-Density Cellular Concrete (1200 – 1800 kg/m³)
This type is suitable for structural applications such as:
   - Load-bearing walls
   - Partition walls
   - Precast load-bearing blocks

2 Medium-Density Cellular Concrete (800 – 1000 kg/m³)
Ideal for non-structural uses such as:
   - Precast non-load-bearing blocks
   - Lightweight wall panels

3 Low-Density Cellular Concrete (400 – 600 kg/m³)
Primarily used for insulation purposes:
   - Thermal and sound insulation
   - Fire-resistant protective layers
   - A better alternative to materials like thermocol, glass wool, and wood wool

Key Benefits of Cellular Concrete

- **Lightweight:** Reduces structural load and transportation costs
- **Thermal and Acoustic Insulation:** Naturally insulating due to air voids
- **Fire and Moisture Resistance:** Improves durability and safety
- **Eco-Friendly:** Utilizes industrial waste like fly ash and reduces raw material use
- **Versatile:** Adaptable for structural, geotechnical, and architectural applications

Advantages of Cellular Concrete

1 **Lightweight Structure**
Cellular concrete significantly reduces the overall weight of a structure. This reduction in dead load minimizes the demand on foundations and makes lifting, handling, and transportation easier, especially in high-rise construction and precast applications.

2 **Excellent Fire Resistance**
The enclosed air voids within cellular concrete act as thermal barriers, enhancing its ability to resist fire. Structures built with this material are non-combustible and can

withstand exposure to high temperatures for extended periods without compromising structural integrity.

3 **Thermal Insulation**
Due to its cellular structure, this concrete offer superior thermal insulation. It helps maintain indoor temperatures and reduces the need for external heating or cooling systems, contributing to energy-efficient buildings.

4 **Acoustic Insulation**
The low density and porous nature of cellular concrete improve sound absorption. It is highly effective in reducing noise transmission, making it ideal for applications requiring sound insulation, such as partition walls and floor systems.

5 **Environmentally Friendly**
Cellular concrete is often made using industrial by-products like fly ash, which helps in waste management and reduces reliance on traditional cement. This makes it an eco-conscious choice for sustainable construction practices.

6 **Cost Efficiency**
The use of foam reduces the volume of cement and aggregates required, thereby lowering material costs. Additionally, incorporating fly ash further cuts down expenses, making cellular concrete an economical option for both small and large-scale projects.

7 **Additional Benefits**

a. **Termite Resistance:** It is not a food source for pests and does not support infestation.

b. **Freeze-Thaw Durability:** Its closed-cell structure resists moisture ingress, offering protection against freeze-thaw cycles.

c. **Ease of Application:** It can be pumped, poured, or cast with ease, even in hard-to-reach areas.

NON-FINES CONCRETE

HIGH-DENSITY CONCRETE

High-Density Concrete, also known as Heavyweight Concrete, is a specialized form of concrete that achieves significantly higher densities—typically in the range of 6000 to 6400 kg/m³—compared to conventional concrete. This type of concrete is primarily designed for applications where radiation shielding, counterweights, or mass damping is essential.

Applications

- Radiation shielding in nuclear power plants, radiology rooms, and particle accelerators
- Counterweights for bridges, cranes, elevators, and dams
- Ballast blocks and underwater pipeline anchors

- Vibration dampers in machinery foundations

Shielding Capability

- High-density concrete is highly effective at absorbing and attenuating harmful radiations such as:
- X-rays
- Gamma rays
- Neutron radiation
- Its dense composition acts as a barrier that reduces the intensity of radiation, making it crucial in health and nuclear safety environments.

High-Density Aggregates

- To attain the desired density, special aggregates with high specific gravity are used, such as:
- Barite ($BaSO_4$)
- Magnetite (Fe_3O_4)
- Hematite (Fe_2O_3)
- Limonite ($FeO(OH)\cdot nH_2O$)
- Goethite
- Ferrophosphorus
- Steel punchings or steel shots
- Iron or lead scrap (where permitted)
- These aggregates have high bulk density and are carefully selected based on their availability, cost, and radiation attenuation properties.

Mix Design Considerations

- Water Content: A relatively higher fixed water content is often necessary to maintain workability due to the high surface area of dense aggregates.
- Cleanliness of Aggregates: Aggregates must be clean and free from contaminants such as oil, grease, clay, and organic matter. Impurities can hinder hydration and weaken the bond between cement paste and aggregates.
- Workability: Due to the weight of the concrete, ensuring uniform mixing and proper compaction is critical.

Special Additives for Radiation Shielding

- To enhance the radiation-shielding properties, boron-based additives such as:
- Colemanite
- Borocalcite

  may be introduced into the mix. These additives are particularly useful for neutron absorption. However, they may influence setting time and early strength, so trial mixes and testing are essential to verify performance.

FIBRE REINFORCED CONCRETE (FRC)

Fibre Reinforced Concrete is a composite construction material made by combining cement, mortar, or concrete with discrete, discontinuous fibres that are uniformly distributed throughout the mixture. The primary purpose of incorporating fibres is to enhance the mechanical properties of concrete, particularly its tensile strength, ductility, crack resistance, and impact resistance.

Characteristics of Fibres

A fibre is a small piece of material that acts as reinforcement within the concrete matrix. Fibres can vary in shape—commonly circular, flat, or irregular—and must possess adequate strength and bonding properties to interact effectively with the cementitious material.

One of the most important parameters used to describe fibres is the Aspect Ratio (l/d):

- Aspect Ratio = Length / Diameter
- Common aspect ratios typically range from 30 to 150 depending on the type and purpose of the fibre.

A higher aspect ratio generally improves the fibre's effectiveness in bridging cracks but may also reduce workability.

Common Types of Fibres Used

- Steel Fibres – Provide excellent tensile and impact resistance
- Glass Fibres – Good for corrosion resistance and surface finish
- Polypropylene Fibres – Improve plastic shrinkage resistance and reduce bleeding
- Carbon Fibres – Offer high tensile strength and chemical resistance
- Natural Fibres (e.g., jute, coir) – Eco-friendly and cost-effective for low-strength applications

Benefits of Fibre Reinforced Concrete

- Improved crack control under both plastic and hardened states
- Enhanced ductility and toughness
- Increased resistance to impact, fatigue, and abrasion
- Reduced permeability and improved durability
- Better performance in seismic zones due to improved energy absorption

NECESSITY OF FIBRE REINFORCED CONCRETE

The incorporation of fibres into concrete is driven by the need to enhance its mechanical and durability properties. Fibre Reinforced Concrete addresses several inherent limitations of conventional concrete, making it highly beneficial in modern construction.

Key Reasons for Using Fibre Reinforced Concrete:

- **Enhanced Tensile Strength**
  Fibres improve the tensile capacity of concrete, which is otherwise weak in tension, thereby reducing the reliance on conventional steel reinforcement for certain applications.
- **Reduction of Porosity**
  The inclusion of fibres minimizes air and water voids within the concrete matrix by interrupting the formation of capillary channels, leading to denser and more impermeable concrete.
- **Improved Durability**
  Fibre reinforcement enhances the long-term durability of concrete by reducing shrinkage cracking and increasing resistance to wear, freeze-thaw cycles, and chemical attacks.
- **Resistance to Creep Deformation**
  Fibres like glass and carbon exhibit excellent resistance to creep, which is a time-dependent deformation under sustained loading. This property is particularly beneficial in load-bearing and long-span structural elements.
- **Thermal Compatibility**
  For optimal performance under temperature variations, it is crucial that both the concrete matrix and the fibres exhibit similar thermal expansion properties. This reduces the risk of thermal stresses and prevents differential movement between the concrete and reinforcement.
- **Crack Arresting Mechanism**
  Closely spaced, uniformly distributed fibres act as micro-reinforcements that intercept and control crack propagation. This contributes to significant improvements in both static strength and dynamic response, such as impact and fatigue resistance.

POLYMER CONCRETE

Polymer Concrete is a type of composite material in which polymers are used either as a complete replacement for traditional cement binders or in combination with cement to enhance performance. When polymers entirely replace Portland cement, the resulting product is called Polymer Concrete (PC). When used in conjunction with cement, the product is known as Polymer Cement Concrete (PCC) or Polymer Modified Concrete (PMC).

Composition

The key components of polymer concrete include:

- **Polymer Binders**
  Thermosetting polymers are most commonly used as binders due to their superior thermal stability, mechanical strength, and chemical resistance. Typical resins include epoxy, polyester, vinyl ester, and urethane. Thermoplastic polymers are rarely used due to their lower performance under heat and stress.
- **Aggregates**
  High-quality aggregates such as **silica**, **quartz**, **granite**, and **limestone** are used to form the bulk of the concrete mix. These aggregates must be:
  - Clean and **free from dust or contaminants**
  - Completely **dry**, to ensure strong bonding with the polymer matrix
    Any moisture or debris can weaken the interfacial bond, thereby reducing the overall strength and durability of the composite.

Uses and Applications

Polymer concrete is valued for its unique performance characteristics and is widely used in both **new construction** and **repair works**. Some common applications include:

- **Structural Repairs**
  Due to its excellent **adhesive properties**, polymer concrete is ideal for patching or repairing both polymer-based and traditional concrete structures.
- **Chemical and Corrosive Environments**
  Its **low permeability** and **high resistance to corrosion** make it suitable for use in:
  - **Sewer systems**
  - **Drainage channels**
  - **Swimming pools**
  - **Chemical storage tanks**
  - **Electrolytic cells** used in the recovery of base metals
- **Industrial Flooring and Precast Components**
  Its durability and resistance to abrasion make it ideal for **industrial floors**, **machine bases**, and **precast components** in aggressive service conditions.

Properties of Polymer Concrete

Polymer concrete exhibits a distinct set of physical, chemical, and mechanical properties that differentiate it from conventional cement-based concrete:

1. High Compressive Strength

- Polymer concrete offers significantly higher compressive strength compared to ordinary Portland cement concrete, making it suitable for heavy-duty structural applications.

2. Excellent Bonding

- It exhibits superior adhesion to both old concrete surfaces and a wide range of substrates, which is beneficial in repair and overlay works.

3. Low Permeability

- Due to the dense polymer matrix, it has very low water absorption and permeability, which protects against moisture ingress, chemical attack, and freeze-thaw damage.

4. Chemical Resistance

- Polymer concrete is highly resistant to acids, alkalis, salts, and solvents, making it ideal for use in chemical plants, sewer systems, and industrial settings.

5. Rapid Curing

- It sets and cures faster than traditional concrete, even under adverse conditions, which reduces downtime during construction or repair work.

6. High Tensile and Flexural Strength

- It has better tensile and flexural strength than regular concrete, reducing the need for heavy reinforcement in certain applications.

7. Improved Durability

- The **long-term durability** is enhanced due to reduced cracking, better resistance to environmental factors, and low shrinkage.

8. Thermal Stability

- Thermosetting resins used in polymer concrete provide good **thermal resistance**, making it suitable for areas with elevated temperatures.

9. Lightweight (Depending on Aggregates)

- When lightweight aggregates are used, polymer concrete can have a **lower density** than traditional concrete, which is advantageous for precast components and retrofitting.

10. Aesthetic Versatility

- It can be easily molded and finished to a variety of textures and appearances, making it useful for architectural and decorative applications.

Types of Polymer Modified Concrete (PMC)

Polymer Modified Concrete refers to cement-based concrete or mortar that has been modified with the addition of polymers to enhance specific properties such as adhesion, tensile strength, and resistance to chemicals and moisture. Based on the type of polymer modifier used, PMC can be broadly classified into the following categories:

1. Latex-Modified Cement Concrete (LMC)

Definition:
This type of PMC is made by adding **polymer latex emulsions** to the concrete or mortar mix. Latex is a stable dispersion of polymer microparticles in water.

Common Latex Polymers Used:

- Styrene-butadiene rubber (SBR)
- Acrylic latex
- Polyvinyl acetate (PVA)

Features:

- Improved bond strength and flexibility
- Better resistance to water penetration and chemical attacks
- Enhanced workability and durability
- Commonly used in bridge deck overlays, patch repairs, and flooring systems

2. Pre-Polymer Modified Cement Concrete (PPMC)

Definition:
In this type, liquid monomers or pre-polymers are added directly to the cement mix. These undergo in-situ polymerization after placement, forming a strong and integrated polymer network within the concrete.

Common Polymers Used:

- Epoxy resins
- Polyester resins
- Urethane-based systems

Features:

- High early strength
- Excellent chemical and abrasion resistance
- Used in industrial floors, sewer linings, repair works, and protective coatings

These types of PMC are selected based on performance requirements, environmental conditions, and specific applications. Both contribute significantly to the longevity and functionality of modern concrete structures.

Prepolymer-Modified Cement Concrete (PPMC)

Prepolymer-Modified Cement Concrete involves the use of liquid resins or prepolymers that undergo in-situ polymerization within the cementitious matrix. Commonly used systems include:

- **Polyester-styrene-based systems**
- **Epoxy resins**
- **Furan resins**

These systems significantly enhance the performance of concrete by modifying its microstructure and bonding characteristics.

Key Characteristics

- **Strength Enhancement:**
  Prepolymer-modified concrete shows a 50% to 100% increase in compressive and flexural strength over conventional concrete.
- **Excellent Adhesion:**
  The concrete develops strong bonding with various substrates, making it ideal for repair applications.
- **Reduced Microcracking:**
  The dense polymer network helps in minimizing micro-crack formation, increasing structural integrity.
- **Lower Water-Cement Ratio:**
  Due to improved workability, less water is required, resulting in a denser and more durable matrix.
- **Pore Filling:**
  The polymers penetrate and fill voids in the mix, contributing to enhanced durability and lower permeability.

Properties of Polymer Modified Concrete (PMC)

1. **Improved Workability**
   Polymer addition makes the mix more cohesive and workable, even with reduced water content.
2. **Higher Crushing Strength**
   Lower water-cement ratio contributes to increased compressive strength.
3. **Stronger Aggregate-Matrix Bond**
   Enhances internal bonding, resulting in better load transfer and durability.

4. **Increased Flexural and Tensile Strength**
   PMC exhibits superior bending and tensile resistance, reducing the need for heavy reinforcement in certain applications.
5. **Higher Air Content**
   PMC typically contains about 3% more entrained air than conventional concrete, which slightly reduces modulus of elasticity but improves freeze-thaw durability.
6. **Extended Setting Time**
   Polymers can delay the setting time, offering more flexibility for placement and finishing.
7. **Improved Abrasion Resistance**
   The tough polymer matrix offers better surface wear resistance.
8. **Superior Freeze-Thaw Durability**
   Ideal for cold regions, PMC withstands repeated freezing and thawing cycles without deterioration.
9. **Reduced Chloride Penetration**
   Low permeability reduces the ingress of harmful ions, enhancing corrosion resistance of reinforcement.
10. **Increased Shear Bond Strength**
    PMC adheres strongly to existing materials, making it suitable for overlays and patching.
11. **Enhanced Ductility**
    PMC can deform more before failure, making it better suited for dynamic loads and seismic areas.

Applications of Polymer Modified Concrete

Polymer modified concretes are used in a wide range of specialized construction and repair applications, such as:

- Structural repairs and overlays on bridges, pavements, and industrial floors
- Waterproofing of basements, swimming pools, and water tanks
- Marine structures and coastal defenses, where resistance to chlorides is critical
- Industrial flooring in chemical plants and warehouses
- Protective coatings for sewer linings and effluent treatment plants
- Precast components requiring enhanced durability and finish quality

HIGH-PERFORMANCE CONCRETE (HPC)

High-Performance Concrete (HPC) is a carefully proportioned concrete that delivers exceptional strength, durability, and workability compared with conventional mixes. While its ingredients are fundamentally the same—cement, water, aggregates, and admixtures—the **type** and dosage of supplementary materials are selected to meet specific performance targets such as low permeability, rapid strength gain, and long service life.

High-Performance Concrete is a mixture whose mechanical and durability properties significantly exceed those of ordinary Portland-cement concrete. Typical benchmarks include compressive strengths well above 60 MPa, very low water absorption, and high resistance to aggressive environments.

Typical Constituents

Component	Purpose
Portland cement	Primary binder
Supplementary cementitious materials (SCMs) — fly ash, silica fume, ground-granulated blast-furnace slag (GGBS)	Reduce permeability, refine pore structure, boost long-term strength
Superplasticizer (high-range water reducer)	Achieves low water–binder ratio (< 0.35) while maintaining good workability
Aggregates (well-graded, low-absorption)	Provide volume stability and strength
Optional admixtures — shrinkage reducers, corrosion inhibitors, fibers	Tailor mix to specific performance requirements

Key Features and Benefits

- **High Strength & Low Permeability**
  Carefully chosen SCMs and a low water–binder ratio produce dense, refined microstructure, raising compressive and flexural strength while drastically reducing chloride and water ingress.

- **Enhanced Durability**
  HPC resists freeze–thaw cycles, alkali-silica reaction, sulfate attack, and carbonation better than conventional concrete, extending the structure's service life and lowering maintenance costs.

- **Improved Workability**
  Superplasticizers allow excellent flow and consolidation even with low water content, facilitating placement in congested reinforcement or complex formwork.

- **Economy Over Life Cycle**
  Although material costs are higher initially, the longer service life, reduced repair frequency, and faster construction (due to earlier strength gain) often make HPC the more economical choice overall.

- **Versatility & Aesthetics**
  With proper mix design and curing, HPC finishes can achieve superior surface quality, color uniformity, and form detail—valuable in architectural concrete.

Why High-Performance Concrete?

Conventional concrete can fall short in severe environments or demanding applications, showing:

- Premature durability issues
- Slow strength development that lengthens construction schedules
- Limited energy absorption in seismic regions
- Challenges in repair and retrofitting

HPC addresses these shortcomings by optimizing strength, durability, toughness, and constructability—and by allowing designers to tailor mixes to the exact performance needs of bridges, high-rise buildings, marine structures, and precast elements.

Performance Is Project-Specific

"High performance" is not a single property; rather, it reflects a mix tailored to its intended role—for example, low heat of hydration for massive pours, rapid strength for precast turnover, or extreme chloride resistance for coastal structures. Therefore, specifications for HPC should always tie performance metrics (strength, permeability, durability tests) to the environmental and structural demands of each project.

SELF-COMPACTING CONCRETE (SCC)

Self-Compacting Concrete (SCC) is a highly flowable, non-segregating concrete that spreads into place and fills formwork under its own weight, without the need for mechanical vibration. It is particularly beneficial in areas where conventional compaction is difficult or impossible due to dense reinforcement or inaccessible locations.

Key Characteristics:

- **High Flowability:** SCC possesses excellent flow characteristics, allowing it to spread and compact by gravity alone.
- **Passing Ability:** It can easily flow through tight spaces between reinforcement without blocking.
- **Stability:** Despite its high fluidity, SCC maintains uniform composition without segregation of aggregates or bleeding.

Advantages of Self-Compacting Concrete (SCC)

Self-Compacting Concrete offers several benefits over conventional concrete due to its ability to flow and compact without external vibration:

1. **Reduced Permeability**
    - The dense and uniform placement of SCC minimizes voids, reducing the permeability of the concrete structure.
2. **Design Flexibility**
    - SCC allows greater freedom in architectural and structural design due to its excellent flowability and ability to fill complex formwork.
3. **Faster Construction**
    - Since SCC does not require mechanical compaction, construction processes are significantly faster.
4. **Elimination of Vibration**
    - The absence of vibration eliminates related issues such as noise, labor fatigue, and the risk of improper compaction.
5. **Ease of Placement**
    - SCC flows easily, even into heavily reinforced areas, simplifying the placing process and reducing the need for skilled labor.
6. **Improved Construction Quality**
    - Homogeneous mixing and better surface finishes enhance the overall quality and appearance of the concrete.
7. **Increased Durability and Reliability**
    - Uniform compaction and low permeability contribute to a longer service life and improved performance of the structure.
8. **Reduced Noise Pollution**
    - Eliminating vibration also minimizes construction site noise, improving working conditions and reducing the risk of hand-arm vibration syndrome.

Disadvantages of Self-Compacting Concrete (SCC)

Despite its advantages, SCC comes with certain limitations that need to be addressed during design and execution:

1. **Lack of Standardized Mix Design Procedures**
    - There is no universally accepted standard for SCC mix design, which may lead to inconsistencies in practice.
2. **Higher Material Costs**
    - SCC typically requires additional admixtures and a higher cementitious content, making it more expensive than conventional concrete.
3. **Increased Need for Trial Mixes**

   - Achieving the desired mix may require several laboratory trials to balance workability and stability.
4. **Demand for Precise Monitoring**
   - SCC requires careful measurement and quality control to maintain its self-compacting properties.
5. **Stricter Material Selection**
   - Only materials that meet tight specifications can be used to ensure performance, limiting flexibility in material sourcing.

Composition of SCC:

To achieve its unique properties, SCC incorporates:

- **Cement** – Ordinary Portland Cement (OPC)
- **Fine Aggregate** – Often finer than in normal concrete
- **Coarse Aggregate** – Well-graded and limited in size
- **Supplementary Cementitious Materials (SCMs):**
  e.g., fly ash, silica fume, or ground granulated blast furnace slag
- **Superplasticizers:** High-range water-reducing admixtures to ensure flowability
- **Viscosity Modifying Agents (VMA):** To enhance cohesion and prevent segregation

Applications of SCC:

- Precast concrete production
- Piles and deep foundations
- Architectural concrete
- Complex or congested reinforcement zones
- Repair works and retrofitting

Tests and Properties of Self-Compacting Concrete (SCC)

The performance of Self-Compacting Concrete (SCC) is primarily defined by its behavior in the **fresh state**. To meet the requirements of SCC, the concrete must demonstrate specific properties that ensure its **flowability, uniformity, and stability** without the use of vibration.

Key Properties of SCC in the Fresh State

1. **Filling Ability**
   - The capacity of SCC to flow and fill formwork completely under its own weight, even in the absence of mechanical vibration.
   - **Importance:** Ensures complete filling of the moulds and encapsulation of reinforcement, which is crucial for structural integrity.
2. **Passing Ability**

- The ability of SCC to flow through congested reinforcement or narrow gaps without causing blockage or segregation.
- **Importance:** Maintains uniform consistency while navigating through complex geometries or heavily reinforced areas.

3. **Segregation Resistance**
   - The resistance of SCC to separate into its individual constituents (i.e., water, cement paste, and aggregates) during flow.
   - **Importance:** Ensures homogeneous mixture throughout the pour, resulting in higher strength and durability.